The
Fundamentals
of the
Chinese Language

—

Writing & Pronunciation

Discovery Publisher

2014, 1st edition, ©Discovery Publisher
2022, 2nd edition, ©Discovery Publisher
All rights reserved.

Author : Brian Stewart

616 Corporate Way
Valley Cottage, New York
www.discoverypublisher.com
editors@discoverypublisher.com
Proudly not on Facebook or Twitter

New York • Paris • Dublin • Tokyo • Hong Kong

PREFACE

The Fundamentals of the Chinese Language is a shortcut to the Chinese written language, not a text book nor a conventional phrase book. Its purpose is to help non-Chinese enjoy the Chinese "Sign Language" that has been developing for 4,000 years. Until the 20th century, it was a language known only to a small minority of Chinese. Few foreigners, unless they were dedicated students, have ever had the courage, tenacity and determination to tackle this language.

Today, most foreign students of the Chinese written language are faced with sentences which are not suited for "first steps". Teachers try to teach beginners both the spoken language and the written language. For example, the phrase: "I am English", which is romanized as "wǒ shì yīng guó rén" (我是英国人.) "Wǒ" is written "我" and has 7 strokes; "yīng" is written "英" and has 8 strokes, etc. However, none of these details provide any explanation of use to a beginner.

Long before I had completed my Chinese studies, I discovered a host of useful explanations and tips which could have expedited my studies. This hard-won knowledge forms the basis for this book. I hope readers will derive as much pleasure from learning something of this venerable language as members of my family have over the last half century.

The idea behind this book was born over sixty years ago when I was studying Chinese in Macau. Since my first teacher spoke no English, I had to learn, as a Chinese child would, by endless practice. The three "P" method (Practice, Practice and more Practice) was an excellent way to develop calligraphy but an inefficient way for an adult to learn. There are many books on this subject, but none have addressed it in the spirit of a wish to help an enthusiastic beginner make a quick, painless entry into the delights of the Chinese written language.

I have frequently tested my theory, so I know that our method works. My daughter Fiona who, because she suffers from Down's Syndrome, was a slow learner, acquired 150 words of written Chinese more quickly than she learned the English alphabet. I have often practiced on fellow British visitors to China, and enjoyed their excitement as they recognized their newly learned Chinese "characters" wherever they went.

We intend to show that, although mastering the Chinese written language may take a lifetime, <u>an understanding of the basics can be grasped in an afternoon</u>, enabling visitors to become at least "partially sighted" as they move around China and Overseas Chinese communities throughout the world.

Although this book is not a text book, we have sprinkled it with tests in order to assist the learning process so that you can, if you wish, review and check your progress. However, it does not pretend to be an academic book. It is no more than an introduction to a fascinating language. An expanded academic version, festooned with footnotes, may follow, but this book has a totally different purpose.

Brian Stewart

TABLE OF CONTENTS

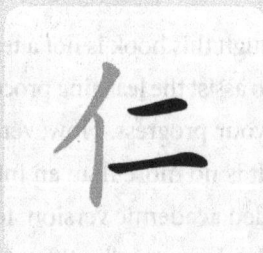

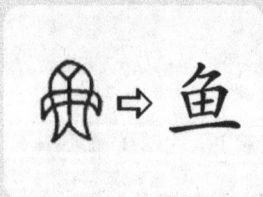

List of Tables

Before you get started...

Before you get started, it might be a good idea to have with you:

- 168 blank index cards or 3x5 note cards; one for each character

- A pen

- A Chinese-English dictionary

LESSON ONE

Definition	One, single, a (article), as soon as, entire, all
Character Evolution	
Stroke Order	
Chinese Proverb	一见钟情

JUMPING IN AT THE SHALLOW END

You most probably already know the following 3 Chinese characters:

- One 一
- Two 二
- Three 三

Number "ten" 十 is also easy to remember. It is a stroke on a "tally stick", marking the passage of ten objects which are being moved in the course of trade.

It is important to start writing immediately. Ideally, you should learn using a brush, which will discourage you from writing strokes in the wrong direction. Also brushes and ink are cheap, and calligraphy is a satisfying pastime. But whatever you use, **practice**.

Most characters are written from the top left corner with the first stroke flowing to the right or downwards:

- One   一   stroke direction   ⋯→

- Two   二   stroke direction   ⋯→   ⋯→

- Three   三   stroke direction   ⋯→   ⋯→   ⋯→

- Ten   十   stroke direction   ⋯→   ↓

There are exceptions, but they are few, and certainly no character is written starting from the bottom right hand corner. Each lesson will show you how to write newly introduced characters and will give you an opportunity to practice.

You will see in the table below we are concerned, as we are throughout, with the composition of the character and its meaning. **Do not worry about the sounds of these symbols.** For the present our concern is only with the structure of the characters[1] not the sounds, which will be discussed later.

Give it a try now!

#	Learn how to write your first 4 Chinese characters			
1	一	一		
2	二	二	二	
3	三	三	三	三
4	十	十	十	

1	一						
2	二						
3	三						
10	十						

1. Throughout the following lessons, we indicate both sets of Chinese characters, the traditional and the simplified sets. The traditional set is marked with "(t: ...)" (see "Simplified and Traditional Chinese" on page 46 for more information on simplified and traditional Chinese sets of characters.)

LIST OF CHINESE CHARACTERS #1 - #27

INTRODUCTION

The characters introduced here will be the pillar of a strong foundation on which we will keep building upon throughout the lessons in this book. First, let us study characters that have similar patterns.

#	CHARACTER	MEANING	DESCRIPTION & EXPLANATION
5	人	Man / person / people	Outline sketch of a body and two legs; a sort of matchstick man
6	个	Individual / this / that / size / classifier for people or objects in general	Pictograph of a bamboo shoot, or the number one (t: 個)
7	大	Big / huge / large / major / great / wide / deep / oldest / eldest	A person with arms outstretched
8	太	Highest / greatest / too (much) / very / extremely	Big 大 (character #7) with an extra dot for emphasis
9	天	Day / sky / heaven	Heaven is the biggest thing any person (character #7) can see
10	从	From / follow / via / passing through / through (a gap) / past / ever	Two people following each other (t: 從)
11	内	Inside / inner / internal / within / interior	A person inside something

#	CHARACTER	MEANING	DESCRIPTION & EXPLANATION
12	肉	Meat / flesh / pulp (of a fruit)	Carcass cut open
13	土	Earth / dust / clay / local / indigenous / unsophisticated	A plant sprouting up through the sub-soil and top soil
14	坐	To sit / to take a seat / to take (a bus, airplane, etc.)	Two men on the ground
15	广	Wide / numerous / to spread	A half-sided large room; a shelter (t: 廣)
16	座	Seat / base / stand	Two people sit in a room (characters #14 and #15)
17	占	To take possession of / to occupy / to constitute / to make up / to account for	A word from someone's mouth
18	点	Drop (of liquid) / point / o'clock / a little / classifier for small indeterminate quantities	Object "standing" (character #17) on a fire, therefore becoming smaller or several (t: 點)
19	店	Inn / shop / store	Standing (character #17) under a shelter (character #15); a store
20	床	Bed / couch / classifier for beds	Wood (character #28) under a shelter (character #15) that makes a bed
21	去	To go / to remove / just passed or elapsed	A person (character #5) (altered) leaving a hole (altered), suggesting motion

#	CHARACTER	MEANING	DESCRIPTION & EXPLANATION
22	在	Located at / to be in / to exist / in the middle of doing sth	A pictograph of a grass root sprouting from earth (character #13)
23	王	King / best or strongest of its type / grand / great	A line above the earth (character #13); an overlord on top of his territory; a king
24	主	Owner or master / host / primary	Pictograph of a king (character #23) with a flame on top
25	住	To live / to dwell / to stay / to reside / to stop	A person still like a master (character #24); to stay
26	国	Country / nation / state / national	A region encompassed (t: 國); now a "jade" inside a boundary
27	因	Cause / reason / because	Outside is a form of boundary including a fence or wall or even a national frontier, this is a radical (will be studied later), inside is a man; a man and his surrounding

Table 1: List of Chinese characters #1 - #27

PRACTICE

Practice, Practice and Practice. Try to find time to practice writing these first 27 characters we have studied so far. The table below shows the order and direction of the strokes for each of the characters presented in Lesson One.

人	丿	人						
个	𠆢	个						

大	一	大	大					
太	大	太						
天	一	二	于	天				
从	丿	人	从	从				
内	丨	冂	内	内				
肉	内	肉	肉					
土	一	十	土					
坐	丿	人	从	坐	坐	坐		
广	丶	亠	广					
座	广	座						
占	丨	卜	占	占	占			
点	占	卢	点	点	点			
店	广	店						
床	广	庐	庄	床	床			
去	土	去	去					
在	一	广	才	在				
王	一	二	干	王				
主	丶	主						
住	丿	亻	住					
国	丨	冂	国	国	国			

因	冂	冈	因						
一	一								
二	一	二							
三	一	二	三						
十	一	十							

If you have a Chinese friend to check your work, so much the better, but careful copying should produce effective results. The more often you write, the more fluid and presentable your characters will be.

We suggest that you write every character you encounter in this book on a card; Chinese writing on one side and the meaning on the other, so that you begin to build a small "dictionary" of cards to which you can add through life. This is a time honored system used by students of Chinese. It has the advantage that the pack can be shuffled and carried in your pocket.

Sample card for 中 (character #151)

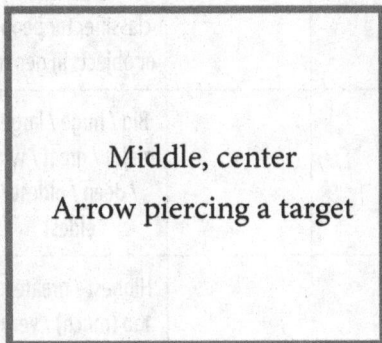

中

Middle, center
Arrow piercing a target

It is suggested that large cards, should be used to leave plenty of room for further notes[1].

LESSON ONE: TEST 1

In the table below, without looking at what we have just studied, write each Chinese character according to its meaning.

1. Memory techniques ("memoria technica"): it is not essential that the student should slavishly adhere to the remarks in Column 4 in the above table ("Description & Explanation"). Any trick will do: it does not matter whether or not the memoria technica has been legitimized by scholars. The only thing that matter is that each new unit under scrutiny should somehow become firmly lodged in the student's memory.
The ambitious student may wish to compete with Father Ricci, the Jesuit in the 18th century, who after decades could astonish the Mandarins with his encyclopaedic knowledge and memory tricks. We lesser mortals can be content if we can lodge a few thousand Chinese characters in our "memory box". It is an interesting hobby for life, which can give at least as much satisfaction to addicts as crossword puzzles.

#	CHARACTER	MEANING	DESCRIPTION & EXPLANATION
5		Man / person / people	Outline sketch of a body and two legs; a sort of matchstick man
6		Individual / this / that / size / classifier for people or objects in general	Pictograph of a bamboo shoot, or the number one (t: 個)
7		Big / huge / large / major / great / wide / deep / oldest / eldest	A person with arms outstretched
8		Highest / greatest / too (much) / very / extremely	Big 大 (character #7) with an extra dot for emphasis

#	CHARACTER	MEANING	DESCRIPTION & EXPLANATION
9		Day / sky / heaven	Heaven is the biggest thing any person (character #7) can see
10		From / follow / via / passing through / through (a gap) / past / ever	Two people following each other (t: 從)
11		Inside / inner / internal / within / interior	A person inside something
12		Meat / flesh / pulp (of a fruit)	Carcass cut open
13		Earth / dust / clay / local / indigenous / unsophisticated	A plant sprouting up through the sub-soil and top soil
14		To sit / to take a seat / to take (a bus, airplane, etc.)	Two men on the ground
15		Wide / numerous / to spread	A half-sided large room; a shelter (t: 廣)
16		Seat / base / stand	Two people sit in a room (characters #14 and #15)
17		To take possession of / to occupy / to constitute / to make up / to account for	A word from someone's mouth

#	CHARACTER	MEANING	DESCRIPTION & EXPLANATION
18		Drop (of liquid) / point / o'clock / a little / classifier for small indeterminate quantities	Object "standing" (character #17) on a fire, therefore becoming smaller or several (t: 點)
19		Inn / shop / store	Standing (character #17) under a shelter (character #15); a store
20		Bed / couch / classifier for beds	Wood (character #28) under a shelter (character #15) that makes a bed
21		To go / to remove / just passed or elapsed	A person (character #5) (altered) leaving a hole (altered), suggesting motion
22		Located at / to be in / to exist / in the middle of doing sth	A pictograph of a grass root sprouting from earth (character #13)
23		King / best or strongest of its type / grand / great	A line above the earth (character #13); an overlord on top of his territory; a king
24		Owner or master / host / primary	Pictograph of a king (character #23) with a flame on top
25		To live / to dwell / to stay / to reside / to stop	A person still like a master (character #24); to stay
26		Country / nation / state / national	A region encompassed (t: 國); now a "jade" inside a boundary

#	CHARACTER	MEANING	DESCRIPTION & EXPLANATION
27		Cause / reason / because	Outside is a form of boundary including a fence or wall or even a national frontier, this is a radical (will be studied later), inside is a man; a man and his surrounding

LESSON ONE: TEST 2

In the table below, without looking at what we have just studied, write the meaning of each Chinese character.

#	CHARACTER	MEANING	DESCRIPTION & EXPLANATION
5	人		Outline sketch of a body and two legs; a sort of matchstick man
6	个		Pictograph of a bamboo shoot, or the number one (t: 個)
7	大		A person with arms outstretched
8	太		Big 大 (character #7) with an extra dot for emphasis
9	天		Heaven is the biggest thing any person (character #7) can see

#	CHARACTER	MEANING	DESCRIPTION & EXPLANATION
10	从		Two people following each other (t: 從)
11	内		A person inside something
12	肉		Carcass cut open
13	土		A plant sprouting up through the sub-soil and top soil
14	坐		Two men on the ground
15	广		A half-sided large room; a shelter (t: 廣)
16	座		Two people sit in a room (characters #14 and #15)
17	占		A word from someone's mouth
18	点		Object "standing" (character #17) on a fire, therefore becoming smaller or several (t: 點)

#	CHARACTER	MEANING	DESCRIPTION & EXPLANATION
19	店		Standing (character #17) under a shelter (character #15); a store
20	床		Wood (character #28) under a shelter (character #15) that makes a bed
21	去		A person (character #5) (altered) leaving a hole (altered), suggesting motion
22	在		A pictograph of a grass root sprouting from earth (character #13)
23	王		A line above the earth (character #13); an overlord on top of his territory; a king
24	主		Pictograph of a king (character #23) with a flame on top
25	住		A person still like a master (character #24); to stay
26	国		A region encompassed (t: 國); now a "jade" inside a boundary
27	因		Outside is a form of boundary including a fence or wall or even a national frontier, this is a radical (will be studied later), inside is a man; a man and his surrounding

HOW TO WRITE CHINESE CHARACTERS

Since you have had a first experience with Chinese characters in
this lesson, it is now time to learn some basic rules about writing
Chinese characters.

STROKE TYPES

Strokes are traditionally classified into 8 basic forms, each appear-
ing in the character "eternally" 永 and listed below according to
their contemporary names:

1 Dian, 点, Dot

2 Heng, 横, Horizontal stroke, left to right

3 Shu, 竖, Vertical stroke, top to bottom

4 Gou, 钩, Hook appended to other strokes

5 Ti, 提, Diagonal stroke, rising from left to right

6 Pie, 撇, Diagonal stroke, falling from right
to left

7 Duan Pie, 短撇, Short diagonal stroke, falling
from right to left

8 Na, 捺, Horizontal stroke, falling from left
to right

These basic strokes are sometimes combined without the pen leav-
ing the paper. In the above example of "eternally", strokes 2-3-4 are
written as one continuous stroke, as are strokes 5-6. Hence in dictionaries this character is indexed as having five separate strokes.

STROKE ORDER

Writing characters in the correct order is essential for the character to look correct. Two basic rules are followed:

1 Top before bottom
2 Left before right

These rules conflict whenever one stroke is to the bottom and left of another. Several additional rules resolve many of these conflicts.

3 Left vertical stroke (usually) before top horizontal stroke

4 Bottom horizontal stroke last

5 Center stroke before side strokes

6 Horizontal strokes before intersecting vertical strokes

7 Left-falling strokes before right-falling strokes

A final rule can contradict the others:

8 Minor strokes (often) last

Despite these conflicts between rules, most students quickly acquire a natural feel for the proper stroke order.

COMPONENT ORDER

Most Chinese characters are combinations of simpler, component characters. Usually the two parts are written at top and bottom or left and right so that the main two stroke order rules readily apply. Occasionally these rules also conflict with respect to components. When one component is at the bottom-left, and the other at the top-right, the top-right component is sometimes written first.

When there are several components, top components are written first.

These rules usually imply each component is written in its entirety before another component is written. Exceptions may arise when one component divides another, encompasses another, or the individual components are no longer discernible in modern writing. If the above is confusing to you, <u>do not panic</u>. It all will make more sense after going through the first two or three lessons.

PRACTICAL CHINESE CORNER

You know 2 characters out of the 3 highlighted. What do you think this celebration is about, a new car, a new song, or a big hotel?

You know 1 character out of the 2 highlighted. Is this grand opening a national event?

From the 2 highlighted characters, is this a well-known finance & economics magazine?

Definition	Two, second, different, binary
Character Evolution	
Stroke Order	
Chinese Proverb	二三其德

THE FORMATION OF CHINESE CHARACTERS

We shall now look at various types of Chinese characters: "pictographs", "ideographs", "combinations" and "radicals". Sometimes the radical will stand alone, sometimes it will be one element in a character, combining several elements.

PICTOGRAPHS

These were originally line drawings but have changed form over thousands of years. Some pictographs, for example, big (character #7 "大" on page 10); follow (character #10 "从" on page 10); wood (character #28 "木" on page 41); mouth, opening (character #45 "口" on page 36); person (character #5 "人" on page 10) need little explanation.

大	从	木	口	人
Character #7	Character #10	Character #28	Character #45	Character #5
Examples of pictographs				

But unfortunately for the student, few pictographs are so obviously linked to their original form.

IDEOGRAPHS

Ideographs suggest an idea or concept, rather than sketching an image. One example is 从, an ideograph you have already met, meaning "to follow". It consists of two 人 people (character #10 "人" on page 10) people following each other.

Another example is 国, country (character #26 "国" on page 12). This combination consists of two elements; 囗 a frontier (see radical "囗" on page 163) and 玉 a piece of jade.

COMBINATIONS

The combination combines elements to make a pictograph or an ideograph. For example, 森 forest (character #30 "森" on page 34), is not a sketch meaning three trees but an ideograph meaning "forest". 休 to rest (character #31 "休" on page 34) combines two pictographs 人 man (character #5 "人" on page 10) and 木 tree (character #28 "本" on page 34), meaning a man resting against a tree.

住	相	休	森	和
Character #25	Character #34	Character #31	Character #30	Character #48
Examples of combinations of elements to make Chinese characters				

RADICALS

The term radical[1] is most commonly used to refer to the section headers of a Chinese dictionary (部首, bù shǒu), also known as a key or classifier. These are used to index Chinese characters in Chinese dictionaries. The indexing system supports Chinese characters throughout the ages, from the Shuōwén Jiézì dictionary (early 2nd century Common Era Chinese dictionary from the Han Dynasty) to modern ones.

The radical element can stand alone, for example, 人 a person (character #5 "人" on page 10). In a combination, it is usually

[1] The term "radical" has been objected to by some scholars, due to widespread confusion over the implications of its coinage. Professor Creel of Chicago University, one of the seminal figures in the Western academic analysis of Chinese, was critical of the use of word "radical"; he preferred the word "key".

found on the left side as in 休 to rest (character #31 "休" on page 34) Sometimes a radical is to be found on the top or on the bottom and, very seldom, on the right.

住	相	休	森	和
Character #25	Character #34	Character #31	Character #30	Character #48
The grayed area of each character shows the radical				

In the Kang Xi dictionary (18th Century), 214 characters were identified as radicals. Such radical characters, when used in a combination, usually give some indication of the meaning. Therefore, radicals can be of considerable help to memory. One of the most commonly seen of all the radicals is known colloquially as "three-dots-water", or 氵. "Three-dots-water" is a shorthand form of the character for water 水. If you see "three-dots-water" on the left of a character, it is certain that the character has some connection with liquid. The characters for "sea" 海, "lake" 湖, "river" 河, "oil" 油, and "alcohol" 酒, all use "three-dots-water" as their radical.

The Kangxi dictionary lists a total of 47,035 characters divided among the 214 radicals. There are seven radicals which form more than 1,000 characters each:

艹	氵	木	扌	口
Grass 1,902	Water 1,595	Tree 1,369	Hand 1,203	Mouth 1,146

小	虫	
Heart 1,115	Insect 1,067	
Seven radicals that form more than 1,000 characters each		

The following radicals usually indicate some common character-istics in their radical:

- The "Grass" radical ⁺⁺ will probably mean that the character has something to do with plants or flowers. Thus, the character for 花 flower shows the phonetic 化 under the radical ⁺⁺.
- The "Tree" radical 木 (character #28 "木" on page 34), will probably mean that the character is about wood, construction, or even machine.
- The "Fire" radical 火 usually indicates that the character has something to do with fire or heat.
- The "Woman" radical 女 (character #53 "女" on page 47), usually indicates, not surprisingly, something female.

Unfortunately for the student, not every combination includes a radical element providing a clue to category; happily, many do conform.

EXAMPLES OF COMMON RADICALS

The table below contains a list of common radicals, with their meaning and example characters. For a complete list of radicals, refer to "List of 214 Kangxi radicals" on page 161.

#	RADICAL	MEANING	EXAMPLE CHARACTERS
1	人(亻)	Man, human	今 从 (仁 休 位)

#	RADICAL	MEANING	EXAMPLE CHARACTERS
2	冫	Ice	冶 冷 冻
3	刀 (刂)	Knife, sword	刀 切
4	口	Mouth, opening	口 可 君 否
5	囗	Enclosure	四 回 因
6	土	Earth	土 在 地 城
7	女	Woman, female	女 好 妻 姓
8	彳	Step	役 彼 得
9	心 (忄小)	Heart	想 (忙 情 性)
10	手 (扌𠂇)	Hand	手 拿 (打 抱)
11	日	Sun, day	日 明 映 晚
12	月	Moon, month, meat	有 服 胀 肺
13	木	Tree	木 相 森 林
14	水 (氵氺)	Water	水 永 (泳 治)
15	火 (灬)	Fire	火 灯 (点 照)
16	疒	Sickness	病 症 痛 癌
17	目	Eye	目 省 眠 眼
18	肉	Meat	胬
19	虫	Insect	蚯 蚓
20	讠	Speech	讲 设 评 试
21	阝	Town, wall	那 邦
22	食 (饣)	Eat, food	餐 (饭 饮)

Table 2: Example of common radicals

LESSON TWO: TEST 1

According to the table "List of Chinese characters #1 - #27" on page 10, write down the radical of each character and select the correct radical definition. See "Test Answer Key 1" on page 171 for answers.

#	RADICAL	MEANING	EXAMPLE
1		☐ Food ☐ Man	从
2		☐ Hand ☐ Insect	打
3		☐ Moon ☐ Sun	明
4		☐ Meat ☐ Table	肺
5		☐ Wood ☐ Meat	相
6		☐ Ice ☐ Water	泳
7		☐ Light ☐ Fire	灯
8		☐ Sickness ☐ Container	病
9		☐ Eye ☐ Moon	眼
10		☐ Meat ☐ Flame	朕
11		☐ Music ☐ Insect	蛇
12		☐ Flower ☐ Ice	冰
13		☐ Speech ☐ Travel	讲
14		☐ Knife ☐ Roof	召
15		☐ Mouth ☐ House	否

PRACTICAL CHINESE CORNER

Looking at the radical of the highlighted character, what do you think this event is about?

Looking at the radical of the highlighted character, what do you thing this week's issue of this magazine is about?

Looking at the radical of the highlighted character, what do you think this competition was about?

Definition	Three, third, several, a few
Character Evolution	三 三 三 三
Stroke Order	一 二 三
Chinese Proverb	三思而行

In this lesson, we will look briefly at the evolution of Chinese characters and add more characters to our list.

EVOLUTION OF CHINESE CHARACTERS

The Chinese language has an extremely ancient system of writing. What is even more stunning is that it went through relatively small amounts of change through its 3500 years of evolution, which is divided into several stages. The table below shows the changes through time for the characters "Fish", "Could", Moon", and "Man".

Chinese Name	English Name	Mandarin	Character Evolution			
			"Fish"	"Could"	"Moon"	"Man"
甲骨文 1200-1050 BC	Bone Script	Jiaguwen				
金文 770 BC-220 BC	Bronze Engraving	Jinwen				
篆书 220 BC-220 AD	Seal Style	Zhuanshu				
隶书 25-220 AD	Clerkly Script	Lishu	魚	雲	月	人
楷书 173 AD	Standard Script	Kaishu	魚	雲	月	人
行书 87 AD	Running Script	Xingshu	魚	雲	月	人
草书 206 BC-8 AD	Cursive Script	Caoshu	魚	雲	月	人

Table 3: Evolution of Chinese characters

Chinese Name	English Name	Mandarin	Character Evolution			
			"Fish"	"Could"	"Moon"	"Man"
简体字 1949 AD	Simplified Script	Jiantizi	鱼	云	月	人

LIST OF CHINESE CHARACTERS #28 - #52

This list introduces frequently used Chinese characters, most of which have their own meaning. They can be also used as radicals to form more complex characters. After this lesson, you should be able to identify more complex characters, even if you haven't studied them yet. Since you have learned about ancient Chinese characters, we will display them whenever available.

#	CHARACTER	ANCIENT FORM	MEANING	DESCRIPTION & EXPLANATION
28	木		Tree / wood	Outline picture of a tree; branches and vertical trunk
29	林		Forest / wood	Two trees (character #28) representing a forest
30	森		Thicket / dense wood	Three trees (character #28) representing many trees and bushes together, a dense forest
31	休		To rest	A person (character #5) resting against or under a tree (character #28)
32	本		Roots or stems of plants / origin / source	Root at the bottom of tree (character #28) trunk
33	目		Eye / item / goal	Originally a pictograph of an eye

#	CHARACTER	ANCIENT FORM	MEANING	DESCRIPTION & EXPLANATION
34	相		Appearance / portrait / to examine	An eye (character #33) looking at a tree (character #28); to examine
35	心		Heart / mind	Human heart with valves and tubes leading from it
36	想		To think / to believe / to want / to miss	To examine (character #34) the mind (character #35); to think
37	日		Sun / day / day of the month	Pictograph of the sun
38	白		White / empty / blank / plain / clear / in vain	Sun 日 (character #37) with mark indicating it is just rising
39	勺		Spoon	Pictograph of a spoon
40	的		Of (possessive)	No short explanation available, but this character is important to know
41	百		Hundred / numerous / all kinds of	One (character #1) and white (character #38) suggesting a large number
42	是		Is / are / am / yes / to be	Under the light of the day (character #37)
43	早		Early / morning	Sun (character #37) rising (suggestion using character #4)
44	昨		Yesterday	Day (character #37) and past

#	CHARACTER	ANCIENT FORM	MEANING	DESCRIPTION & EXPLANATION
45	口	𦥑	Mouth / Entrance	A mouth; an opening such as a doorway or entrance; as usual the circle has been converted to a square which is more convenient for a person writing with a brush
46	喝	喝	To drink / to shout (a command)	A mouth (character #45) with 曷 phonetic (phonetics will be discussed later)
47	禾	禾	Millet / cereal / grain	A grain of wheat on top of a plant
48	和	和	And / together with / sum / union / peace / harmony	Harmony between grain and mouth
49	香	香	Fragrant / sweet smelling / savory or appetizing	Millet 禾 (character #47) and sweet 甘 (now 日)
50	吃	吃	To eat / to absorb / to suffer / to exhaust	A mouth (character #45) with a pictograph giving the impression of absorbing something
51	品	品	Article / goods / rank / character / disposition	Three boxes (character #47) representing a pile of commercial goods; can be seen on many business signboards
52	回	回	To go back / to answer	Two concentric shapes representing a return journey

Table 4: List of Chinese characters #28 - #52

LESSON THREE: STROKE ORDER & PRACTICE

The table below shows the order and direction of the strokes for each of the characters presented in this lesson. Now it's your turn to practice.

木	一	十	木						
林	木	林							
森	木	森	森						
休	亻	休							
本	木	本							
目	冂	冃	冃	目					
相	木	相							
心	丶	儿	心						
想	相	想							
日	丨	冂	冃	日					
白	丶	白							
勺	丿	勹	勺						
的	白	的							
百	一	百							
是	旦	旦	早	是	昰	是			
早	日	旦	早						

昨	日	旷	旷	昨	昨				
口	丨	冂	口						
喝	口	叩	唱	喝	喝				
禾	一	二	千	禾	禾				
和	禾	和							
香	禾	香							
吃	口	吖	吖	吃					
品	口	吕	品						
回	冂	向	回						

LESSON THREE: TEST 1

In the table below, without looking at what we have just studied, write each Chinese character according to its meaning.

#	CHARACTER	MEANING	DESCRIPTION & EXPLANATION
28		Tree / wood	Outline picture of a tree; branches and vertical trunk
29		Forest / wood	Two trees (character #28) representing a forest
30		Thicket / dense wood	Three trees (character #28) representing many trees and bushes together, a dense forest

#	CHARACTER	MEANING	DESCRIPTION & EXPLANATION
31		To rest	A person (character #5) resting against or under a tree (character #28)
32		Roots or stems of plants / origin / source	Root at the bottom of tree (character #28) trunk
33		Eye / item / goal	Originally a pictograph of an eye
34		Appearance / portrait / to examine	An eye (character #33) looking at a tree (character #28); to examine
35		Heart / mind	Human heart with valves and tubes leading from it
36		To think / to believe / to want / to miss	To examine (character #34) the mind (character #35); to think
37		Sun / day / day of the month	Pictograph of the sun
38		White / empty / blank / plain / clear / in vain	Sun 日 (character #37) with mark indicating it is just rising
39		Spoon	Pictograph of a spoon

#	CHARACTER	MEANING	DESCRIPTION & EXPLANATION
40		Of (possessive)	No short explanation available, but this character is important to know
41		Hundred / numerous / all kinds of	One (character #1) and white (character #38) suggesting a large number
42		Is / are / am / yes / to be	Under the light of the day (character #37)
43		Early / morning	Sun (character #37) rising (suggestion using character #4)
44		Yesterday	Day (character #37) and past
45		Mouth / Entrance	A mouth; an opening such as a doorway or entrance; as usual the circle has been converted to a square which is more convenient for a person writing with a brush
46		To drink / to shout (a command)	A mouth (character #45) with 曷 phonetic (phonetics will be discussed later)
47		Millet / cereal / grain	A grain of wheat on top of a plant
48		And / together with / sum / union / peace / harmony	Harmony between grain and mouth

#	CHARACTER	MEANING	DESCRIPTION & EXPLANATION
49		Fragrant / sweet smelling / savory or appetizing	Millet 禾 (character #47) and sweet 甘 (now 日)
50		To eat / to absorb / to suffer / to exhaust	A mouth (character #45) with a pictograph giving the impression of absorbing something
51		Article / goods / rank / character / disposition	Three boxes (character #45) representing a pile of commercial goods; can be seen on many business signboards
52		To go back / to answer	Two concentric shapes representing a return journey

LESSON THREE: TEST 2

In the table below, without looking at what we have just studied, write the meaning of each Chinese character.

#	CHARACTER	MEANING	DESCRIPTION & EXPLANATION
28	木		Outline picture of a tree; branches and vertical trunk
29	林		Two trees (character #28) representing a forest
30	森		Three trees (character #28) representing many trees and bushes together, a dense forest

#	CHARACTER	MEANING	DESCRIPTION & EXPLANATION
31	休		A person (character #5) resting against or under a tree (character #28)
32	本		Root at the bottom of tree (character #28) trunk
33	目		Originally a pictograph of an eye
34	相		An eye (character #33) looking at a tree (character #28); to examine
35	心		Human heart with valves and tubes leading from it
36	想		To examine (character #34) the mind (character #35); to think
37	日		Pictograph of the sun
38	白		Sun 日 (character #37) with mark indicating it is just rising
39	勺		Pictograph of a spoon
40	的		No short explanation available, but this character is important to know
41	百		One (character #1) and white (character #38) suggesting a large number
42	是		Under the light of the day (character #37)

#	CHARACTER	MEANING	DESCRIPTION & EXPLANATION
43	早		Sun (character #37) rising (suggestion using character #4)
44	昨		Day (character #37) and past
45	口		A mouth; an opening such as a doorway or entrance; as usual the circle has been converted to a square which is more convenient for a person writing with a brush
46	喝		A mouth (character #45) with 曷 phonetic (phonetics will be discussed later)
47	禾		A grain of wheat on top of a plant
48	和		Harmony between grain and mouth
49	香		Millet 禾 (character #47) and sweet 甘 (now 日)
50	吃		A mouth (character #45) with a pictograph giving the impression of absorbing something
51	品		Three boxes (character #45) representing a pile of commercial goods; can be seen on many business signboards
52	回		Two concentric shapes representing a return journey

PRACTICAL CHINESE CORNER

香水之城

Looking at the highlighted character, what's the main characteristic of this village, its landscape, blue sky, or fragrance?

隆福寺小吃店

Looking at the 2 highlighted characters, what is this place, a perfume shop, a small restaurant, or a cinema?

体验 "国产森林人"
陆风X8质量做工评测

Looking at the 3 highlighted characters, what type of car is the vehicle in the picture, luxury, 4-wheel-drive, or sports car?

LESSON FOUR

Definition	Four			
Character Evolution	三	𦥔	𦥑	四
Stroke Order	丨	冂	冋	四 四
Chinese Proverb	四海为家			

SIMPLIFIED AND TRADITIONAL CHINESE

In the 20th century, written Chinese divided into two canonical forms, called 简体字 jiǎntǐzì (simplified Chinese) and 繁体字 fántǐzì (traditional Chinese). Simplified Chinese was developed in mainland China in order to make the characters faster to write (especially as some characters had as many as a few dozen strokes) and easier to memorize.

讓	⇨	让
24 Strokes		**5 Strokes**
Traditional		**Simplified**

The simplified forms have fewer strokes than the traditional forms. For instance, traditional 讓 "allow", as shown above, is simplified to 让, in which the phonetic on the right side is reduced from 17 strokes to just three. (The "speech" radical 讠 on the left has also been simplified.)

However, the same phonetic as 讓 is used in its full form, even in simplified Chinese. In such characters as 壤 "soil" and 齉 "snuffle", these forms remained uncontracted because they were relatively uncommon and would therefore represent a negligible stroke reduction.

On the other hand, some simplified forms are simply calligraphic abbreviations of long standing, as for example 万 "ten thousand", for which the traditional Chinese form is 萬.

Simplified Chinese is standard in the People's Republic of China, Singapore, and Malaysia. Traditional Chinese is retained in Hong Kong, Taiwan, Macau and overseas Chinese communities (except Singapore and Malaysia).

LIST OF CHINESE CHARACTERS #53 - #76

This list introduces frequently used Chinese characters, most of which have their own meaning. They can be also used as radicals to form more complex characters. After this lesson, you should be able to identify more complex characters, even if you haven't studied them yet.

#	CHARACTER	ANCIENT FORM	MEANING	DESCRIPTION & EXPLANATION
53	女		Female / woman	Pictograph of a kneeling woman
54	了		Gives a notion of time	No short explanation available, but this character is important to know
55	子		Son / child / seed / small thing	Child wrapped in swaddling clothes
56	好		Good / well / proper / good to	Woman (character #53) and baby (character #55) together, suggesting good things
57	安		Content / calm / still / quiet / safe / secure	One woman (character #53) under a roof, suggesting peace
58	字		Letter / symbol / character	Traditionally the written word was treated with reverence; here it is represented by a baby (character #55) under a roof
59	家		Home / family / classifier for families or businesses	A roof with pigs, suggesting home

#	CHARACTER	ANCIENT FORM	MEANING	DESCRIPTION & EXPLANATION
60	妈	爤	Mother	A woman (character #53) with 马 (character #163) phonetic (phonetics will be discussed later) (t: 媽)
61	吗	暇	Used as a question mark	A mouth (character #45) with 马 (character #163) phonetic (phonetics will be discussed later) (t: 嗎)
62	骂	羼	To scold / abuse	Two mouths (character #45) with 马 (character #163) phonetic (phonetics will be discussed later), suggesting shouting (t: 罵)
63	石	ᄀ	Rock / stone	A boulder under a cliff as in a quarry
64	码	曘	Number / code / weight	A stone (character #63) with 马 (character #163) phonetic (phonetics will be discussed later) (t: 碼)
65	田	田	Field / farm	Land divided into plots
66	力	∖	Power / force / strength	Pictograph suggesting strength (t: 辦)
67	办	蘨	To do / to manage / to handle	Using strength (character #66) to produce something (hence the two dots)
68	为	偤	Because of / as / to take sth as / to act as	(t: 為) no short explanation available, but this character is important to know
69	男	毗	Male	Field (character #65) and strength (character #66), suggesting men's work
70	果	ᄬ	Fruit	Fruits on top of a tree 木 (character #28)

#	CHARACTER	ANCIENT FORM	MEANING	DESCRIPTION & EXPLANATION
71	门	門	Door, gate	Pictograph of a double door (t: 門)
72	们	㥧	Plural marker for pronouns	Person with 门 (character #71) phonetic (phonetics will be discussed later), suggesting plural (t: 們)
73	问	問	Ask	A mouth (character #45) at the door (character #71) asking a question (t: 問)
74	间	間	Between / among / space	A ray of light showing through the door (character #71) (t: 間)
75	买	買	To buy / to purchase	Originally a net/bag containing money that would be used to buy things (t: 買)
76	卖	賣	To sell / to betray / to spare no effort	Outward purchasing (character #75) (t: 賣)

Table 5: List of Chinese characters #53 - #76

LESSON FOUR: STROKE ORDER & PRACTICE

The table below shows the order and direction of the strokes for each of the characters presented in this lesson. Now it's your turn to practice.

女	女	く	女					
了	㇇	了						
子	了	子						
好	女	好						
安	丶	宀	宀	安				

字	宀	字						
家	宀	宀	宀	宁	豖	家	家	
妈	女	奵	妈	妈				
吗	口	吗						
骂	口	吅	骂					
石	一	丆	石					
码	石	码						
田	冂	田	田					
力	𠃌	力						
办	力	力	办					
为	丶	丷	为	为				
男	田	男						
果	日	果						
门	丶	冂	门					
们	亻	们						
问	门	问						
间	门	间						
买	乛	乛	乛	买				
卖	十	卖						

LESSON FOUR: TEST 1

In the table below, without looking at what we have just studied, write each Chinese character according to its meaning.

#	CHARACTER	MEANING	DESCRIPTION & EXPLANATION
53		Female / woman	Pictograph of a kneeling woman
54		Gives a notion of time	No short explanation available, but this character is important to know
55		Son / child / seed / small thing	Child wrapped in swaddling clothes
56		Good / well / proper / good to	Woman (character #53) and baby (character #55) together, suggesting good things
57		Content / calm / still / quiet / safe / secure	One woman (character #53) under a roof, suggesting peace
58		Letter / symbol / character	Traditionally the written word was treated with reverence; here it is represented by a baby (character #55) under a roof
59		Home / family / classifier for families or businesses	A roof with pigs, suggesting home
60		Mother	A woman (character #53) with 马 (character #163) phonetic (phonetics will be discussed later) (t: 媽)

#	CHARACTER	MEANING	DESCRIPTION & EXPLANATION
61		Used as a question mark	A mouth (character #45) with 马 (character #163) phonetic (phonetics will be discussed later) (t: 嗎)
62		To scold / abuse	Two mouths (character #45) with 马 (character #163) phonetic (phonetics will be discussed later), suggesting shouting (t: 罵)
63		Rock / stone	A boulder under a cliff as in a quarry
64		Number / code / weight	A stone (character #63) with 马 (character #163) phonetic (phonetics will be discussed later) (t: 碼)
65		Field / farm	Land divided into plots
66		Power / force / strength	Pictograph suggesting strength (t: 鞣)
67		To do / to manage / to handle	Using strength (character #66) to produce something (hence the two dots)
68		Because of / as / to take sth as / to act as	(t: 為) no short explanation available, but this character is important to know

#	CHARACTER	MEANING	DESCRIPTION & EXPLANATION
69		Male	Field (character #65) and strength (character #66), suggesting men's work
70		Fruit	Fruits on top of a tree 木 (character #28)
71		Door, gate	Pictograph of a double door (t: 門)
72		Plural marker for pronouns	Person with 门 (character #71) phonetic (phonetics will be discussed later), suggesting plural (t: 們)
73		Ask	A mouth (character #45) at the door (character #71) asking a question (t: 問)
74		Between / among / space	A ray of light showing through the door (character #71) (t: 間)
75		To buy / to purchase	Originally a net/bag containing money that would be used to buy things (t: 買)
76		To sell / to betray / to spare no effort	Outward purchasing (character #75) (t: 賣)

LESSON FOUR: TEST 2

In the table below, without looking at what we have just studied, write the meaning of each Chinese character.

#	CHARACTER	MEANING	DESCRIPTION & EXPLANATION
53	女		Pictograph of a kneeling woman
54	了		No short explanation available, but this character is important to know
55	子		Child wrapped in swaddling clothes
56	好		Woman (character #53) and baby (character #55) together, suggesting good things
57	安		One woman (character #53) under a roof, suggesting peace
58	字		Traditionally the written word was treated with reverence; here it is represented by a baby (character #55) under a roof
59	家		A roof with pigs, suggesting home
60	妈		A woman (character #53) with 马 (character #163) phonetic (phonetics will be discussed later) (t: 媽)

#	CHARACTER	MEANING	DESCRIPTION & EXPLANATION
61	吗		A mouth (character #45) with 马 (character #163) phonetic (phonetics will be discussed later) (t: 嗎)
62	骂		Two mouths (character #45) with 马 (character #163) phonetic (phonetics will be discussed later), suggesting shouting (t: 罵)
63	石		A boulder under a cliff as in a quarry
64	码		A stone (character #63) with 马 (character #163) phonetic (phonetics will be discussed later) (t: 碼)
65	田		Land divided into plots
66	力		Pictograph suggesting strength (t: 辦)
67	办		Using strength (character #66) to produce something (hence the two dots)
68	为		(t: 為) no short explanation available, but this character is important to know
69	男		Field (character #65) and strength (character #66), suggesting men's work
70	果		Fruits on top of a tree 木 (character #28)
71	门		Pictograph of a double door (t: 門)

#	CHARACTER	MEANING	DESCRIPTION & EXPLANATION
72	们		Person with 门 (character #71) phonetic (phonetics will be discussed later), suggesting plural (t: 們)
73	问		A mouth (character #45) at the door (character #71) asking a question (t: 問)
74	间		A ray of light showing through the door (character #71) (t: 間)
75	买		Originally a net/bag containing money that would be used to buy things (t: 買)
76	卖		Outward purchasing (character #75) (t: 賣)

PRACTICAL CHINESE CORNER

男 女
← →
TOILETS

Which direction should you go?

Looking at the highlighted character, what does this shop mainly sell? (Remark: you already know 4 out the 5 characters above)

回家

Where is this young child going?

LESSON FIVE

Definition	Five
Character Evolution	𝕏 ⊠ ⊠ 五
Stroke Order	一 丁 丏 五
Chinese Proverb	五湖四海

LOOKING UP CHINESE CHARACTERS IN A CHINESE DICTIONARY

BY RADICALS

Traditionally, Chinese dictionaries have been organized according to visual elements of the characters. These elements are known as radicals. This is a very rational approach since most Chinese characters are not phonetic (i.e., you cannot tell how they are pronounced simply by looking at them). Under each character, the dictionary includes compounds and phrases that begin with that character. For example, the term for China is Zhongguo 中国, and this appears under the character zhong 中.

BY STROKE COUNT

Many dictionaries (especially specialist dictionaries) index characters according to a stroke number index. In such dictionaries, one finds the characters by counting the total number of strokes and then looking under that number. Because there are many characters with 5 – 13 strokes, the list is further separated according to the type of stroke used for the character's first stroke. There are five of these: a horizontal stroke ⼀, a vertical stroke ｜, a slash ノ, a dot 丶, and a hooked stroke ⼄.

BY SOUND

The bodies of modern mainland dictionaries tend to be organized according to the pronunciation as recorded in the pinyin system (see "Dialects, sounds, spelling and borrowings for phonetic reasons" on page 110.) This makes the dictionary much quicker to use if you already know how to pronounce the character you are seeking, a common situation when you are looking for a new compound that begins with a familiar first character.

LIST OF CHINESE CHARACTERS #77 - #99

We have not introduced the sound for each character yet, but for each of them presented in this lesson, try to look up its definition in a Chinese dictionary using the Radical Index or the Stroke Count Index. This exercise will familiarize you with stroke counts and radicals, which is a particularly good memorization exercise.

#	CHARACTER	ANCIENT FORM	MEANING	DESCRIPTION & EXPLANATION
77	又	彐	(Once) again / also / both... and... / again	Pictograph suggesting a back and forth movement; also representing a right hand
78	双	雙	Two / double / pair / both	Two 又 (character #77), suggesting double (t: 雙)
79	友	㸚	Friend / friendly	Two right hands (altered) working together, suggesting friendship
80	没	㳂	(Negative prefix for verbs) / have not / not	No short explanation available, but this character is important to know (t: 沒)
81	刀	刁	Knife	A hatchet (very short handled)
82	米	𝀜	Rice	Two grains on top of a tree 木 (character #28), a plant
83	来	朿	To come / to arrive / to come round	Pictograph of wheat (character #46) hanging, suggesting "coming" or "has come" (t: 來)
84	粉	𥽿	Powder / noodles or pasta / pink	Knife (character #81) cutting rice grains (character #82), representing powder

#	CHARACTER	ANCIENT FORM	MEANING	DESCRIPTION & EXPLANATION
85	水	氺	Water / river / liquid	Streams flowing together
86	冰	冰	Ice	Ice radical 冫 and water 水 (character #85)
87	汁	汁	Juice	Water (character #85) with 十 (character #4) phonetic (phonetics will be discussed later)
88	千	千	Kilo, thousand	Ten 十 (character #4) lifespans of a person 人 (character #5)
89	开	開	To open / to start / to turn on / to boil	No short explanation available, but this character is important to know (t: 開)
90	古	古	Ancient / old	Ten 十 (character #4) and mouths 口 (character #45), suggesting ten generations
91	舌	舌	Tongue	A mouth (character #45) with object emerging; a tongue
92	话	話	Language / word	Language radical 讠 and tongue 舌 (character #91), suggesting words (t: 話)
93	活	活	To live / alive / living / work	Water radical 氵 with 舌 (character #91) phonetic (phonetics will be discussed later), suggesting vitality
94	月	☽	Month / moon	Pictograph of a crescent moon

#	CHARACTER	ANCIENT FORM	MEANING	DESCRIPTION & EXPLANATION
95	朋	拜	Friend	Two moons (character #94), suggesting friendship
96	明	𥅆	Clear / bright / to understand	Sun and moon together representing brightness
97	有	𠂇	To have / there is / there are / to exist	Pictograph of a hand (character #77) holding something
98	今	亼	Today / modern / present / current	Pictograph of an ancient character suggesting union, now, the present
99	冷	𤺄	Cold	Ice radical 冫 (see character #86) with 令 phonetic (phonetics will be discussed later)

Table 6: List of Chinese characters #77 - #99

LESSON FIVE: STROKE ORDER & PRACTICE

The table below shows the order and direction of the strokes for each of the characters presented in this lesson. Now it's your turn to practice.

又	𠃌	又						
双	又	双						
友	𠂇	友						
没	丶	冫	氵	氵	沕	没		

刀	𠃌	刀						
米	丶	丷	丷	半	米	米		
来	一	来						
粉	米	米	料	粉				
水	亅	刂	水	水				
冰	丶	冫	冰					
汁	氵	汁						
千	一	千						
开	一	二	开	开				
古	十	古						
舌	一	舌						
话	丶	讠	话					
活	氵	活						
月	丿	刀	月	月				
朋	月	朋						
明	日	明						
有	𠂇	有						
今	人	亼	今					
冷	冫	冷	冷					

LESSON FIVE: TEST 1

In the table below, without looking at what we have just studied, write each Chinese character according to its meaning.

#	CHARACTER	MEANING	DESCRIPTION & EXPLANATION
77		(Once) again / also / both... and... / again	Pictograph suggesting a back and forth movement; also representing a right hand
78		Two / double / pair / both	Two 又 (character #77), suggesting double (t: 雙)
79		Friend / friendly	Two right hands (altered) working together, suggesting friendship
80		(Negative prefix for verbs) / have not / not	No short explanation available, but this character is important to know (t: 沒)
81		Knife	A hatchet (very short handled)
82		Rice	Two grains on top of a tree 木 (character #28), a plant
83		To come / to arrive / to come round	Pictograph of wheat (character #46) hanging, suggesting "coming" or "has come" (t: 來)
84		Powder / noodles or pasta / pink	Knife (character #81) cutting rice grains (character #82), representing powder

#	CHARACTER	MEANING	DESCRIPTION & EXPLANATION
85		Water / river / liquid	Streams flowing together
86		Ice	Ice radical 冫 and water 水 (character #85)
87		Juice	Water (character #85) with 十 (character #4) phonetic (phonetics will be discussed later)
88		Kilo, thousand	Ten 十 (character #4) lifespans of a person 人 (character #5)
89		To open / to start / to turn on / to boil	No short explanation available, but this character is important to know (t: 開)
90		Ancient / old	Ten 十 (character #4) and mouths 口 (character #45), suggesting ten generations
91		Tongue	A mouth (character #45) with object emerging; a tongue
92		Language / word	Language radical 讠 and tongue 舌 (character #91), suggesting words (t: 話)

#	CHARACTER	MEANING	DESCRIPTION & EXPLANATION
93		To live / alive / living / work	Water radical 氵 with 舌 (character #91) phonetic (phonetics will be discussed later), suggesting vitality
94		Month / moon	Pictograph of a crescent moon
95		Friend	Two moons (character #94), suggesting friendship
96		Clear / bright / to understand	Sun and moon together representing brightness
97		To have / there is / there are / to exist	Pictograph of a hand (character #77) holding something
98		Today / modern / present / current	Pictograph of an ancient character suggesting union, now, the present
99		Cold	Ice radical 冫 (see character #86) with 令 phonetic (phonetics will be discussed later)

LESSON FIVE: TEST 2

In the table below, without looking at what we have just studied, write the meaning of each Chinese character.

#	CHARACTER	MEANING	DESCRIPTION & EXPLANATION
77	又		Pictograph suggesting a back and forth movement; also representing a right hand
78	双		Two 又 (character #77), suggesting double (t: 雙)
79	友		Two right hands (altered) working together, suggesting friendship
80	没		No short explanation available, but this character is important to know (t: 沒)
81	刀		A hatchet (very short handled)
82	米		Two grains on top of a tree 木 (character #28), a plant
83	来		Pictograph of wheat (character #46) hanging, suggesting "coming" or "has come" (t: 來)
84	粉		Knife (character #81) cutting rice grains (character #82), representing powder
85	水		Streams flowing together

#	CHARACTER	MEANING	DESCRIPTION & EXPLANATION
86	冰		Ice radical 冫 and water 水 (character #85)
87	汁		Water (character #85) with 十 (character #4) phonetic (phonetics will be discussed later)
88	千		Ten 十 (character #4) lifespans of a person 人 (character #5)
89	开		No short explanation available, but this character is important to know (t: 開)
90	古		Ten 十 (character #4) and mouths 口 (character #45), suggesting ten generations
91	舌		A mouth (character #45) with object emerging; a tongue
92	话		Language radical 讠 and tongue 舌 (character #91), suggesting words (t: 話)
93	活		Water radical 氵 with 舌 (character #91) phonetic (phonetics will be discussed later), suggesting vitality
94	月		Pictograph of a crescent moon
95	朋		Two moons (character #94), suggesting friendship
96	明		Sun and moon together representing brightness

#	CHARACTER	MEANING	DESCRIPTION & EXPLANATION
97	有		Pictograph of a hand (character #77) holding something
98	今		Pictograph of an ancient character suggesting union, now, the present
99	冷		Ice radical 冫 (see character #86) with 令 phonetic (phonetics will be discussed later)

PRACTICAL CHINESE CORNER

Looking at the 2 highlighted characters, what is the message given in the above picture?

Looking at the 2 highlighted characters, what is the product analyzed in this financial report?

Looking at the highlighted characters "粉", what is this man most probably going to do?

LESSON SIX

六

Definition	Six
Character Evolution	介　介　凸　六
Stroke Order	丶　亠　宀　六
Chinese Proverb	六六大顺

ARE "CHARACTERS", "WORDS"?

Characters are the most significant unit of the written language for Chinese speakers. Ordinary Chinese discuss or analyze their language in terms of characters (字). Sentences effectively consist of unbroken strings of single-syllable characters, each having their own particular meanings. For this reason, Chinese is popularly regarded as a language composed exclusively of single-syllable words.

While this perception was largely true for the Classical language, in the modern language the situation is not so simple.

There are many monosyllabic words in Chinese, just as there are in English.

Some examples are:

WORD	MEANING	WORD	MEANING
山	Mountain	狗	Dog
人	Person	快	Quick, fast
吃	To eat	看	To see

But not every character can be regarded as a single word. There are huge number of words that consist of multiple syllables, mostly two syllables.

Inherently, multiple-syllable words cannot be split into smaller units. Some examples are:

WORD	MEANING
葡萄	Grape
玫瑰	Rose
玻璃	Glass

LIST OF CHINESE CHARACTERS #100 - #130

We have not introduced the sound for each character yet, but for each of them presented in this lesson, try to look up its definition in a Chinese dictionary using the Radical Index or the Stroke Count Index. This exercise will familiarize you with stroke counts and radicals, which is a particularly good memorization exercise.

#	CHARACTER	ANCIENT FORM	MEANING	DESCRIPTION & EXPLANATION
100	户		A household / door / family	Pictograph of a door leaf representing a household
101	万		Ten thousand / a great number	The traditional form is: 萬; the modern form has no direct connection with the meaning of its original form
102	方		Direction / square / upright / one side / place	Pictograph of a man giving directions
103	房		House / room	Pictograph of a household (character #100) and a place (character #102)
104	上		Up / above	A symbol of something on top or pointing upwards
105	下		Down / below	The reverse of character #104; above
106	卡		Card / to stop / to block	Pictograph of a device used to stop something from going up (character #104) or down (character #105), representing a card

#	CHARACTER	ANCIENT FORM	MEANING	DESCRIPTION & EXPLANATION
107	直		Straight / vertical / frank / to straighten	Ten (character #4), eyes (character #33) looking at something, suggesting straight, direct
108	具		Tool / ability / to possess	Pictograph representing a tool
109	真		Really / truly / indeed / real / true / genuine	The early pictograph suggests something that has been unveiled, suggesting reality
110	寸		A unit of length / inch / thumb	Pictograph a hand with a tool, representing a measure or an unit
111	对		Right / pair / to be opposite / to face / versus / for / vertical	Hand (character #77) and measure (character #110), suggesting "right" (t: 對)
112	过		Experience action marker / to cross / to go over / to pass (time)	Movement radical 辶 and measure (character #110), suggesting time (t: 過)
113	时		O'clock / time / when / hour / period	Day of the month (character #37) and measure (character #110), suggesting time (t: 時)
114	村		Village	Wood (character #28) with 寸 phonetic (phonetics will be discussed later)
115	树		Tree	Wood (character #28) and vertical (character #111) (t: 樹)
116	贝		Shellfish / currency	Pictograph of a shell (t: 貝)

#	CHARACTER	ANCIENT FORM	MEANING	DESCRIPTION & EXPLANATION
117	见		To see / to meet / to appear	An eye 目 (character #33) on top of a person 儿; (t: 見)
118	贵		Expensive / noble	Pictograph of a basket of money (shells) (t: 貴)
119	现		Appear / present / existing / current	Jade 玉 that can be seen (character #117) (t: 現)
120	立		Standing, upright	Person standing in upright position on the ground
121	产		To give birth / to reproduce / to produce / product	The traditional form 產 suggested birth with 厂 phonetic (phonetics will be discussed later)
122	位		Position / location / place / seat	A person (character #5) standing in assigned position (character #120)
123	站		Station / to stand / to halt / to stop	Stand with 占 (character #17) phonetic (phonetics will be discussed later)
124	小		Small / tiny / few / young	An object broken into two small bits
125	少		Few / little / lack; young	Take away from already small (character #124)
126	尖		Point (of needle) / sharp / pointed	Small 小 (character #124) and big 大 (character #7)
127	夕		Dusk / evening	Pictograph of a crescent moon

#	CHARACTER	ANCIENT FORM	MEANING	DESCRIPTION & EXPLANATION
128	多	多	Many / much / a lot of	Many moons (character #127)
129	名	𥅀	Name / noun / famous	Identify in the dark (evening, character #127), suggesting name
130	句	句	Sentence / clause / phrase	Pictograph suggesting words from a mouth (character #45) that form a sentence

Table 7: List of Chinese characters #100 - #130

LESSON SIX: STROKE ORDER & PRACTICE

The table below shows the order and direction of the strokes for each of the characters presented in this lesson. Now it's your turn to practice.

户	丶	㇕	㇕	户					
万	一	丁	万						
方	丶	方							
房	户	房							
上	丨	卜	上						
下	一	下	丁						
卡	上	卡	卡						
直	一	十	肖	直					
具	目	具	具						

真	直	真	真					
寸	一	寸	寸					
对	又	对						
过	寸	寸	讨	过				
时	日	时						
村	木	村						
树	木	树						
贝	丨	冂	贝	贝				
见	贝	见						
贵	一	虫	虫	贵				
现	王	现						
立	丶	亠	产	立	立			
产	立	产						
位	亻	位						
站	立	站						
小	亅	小	小					
少	小	少						
尖	小	尖						
夕	丿	夕	夕					
多	夕	多						

名	夕	名							
句	勹	句							

LESSON SIX: TEST 1

In the table below, without looking at what we have just studied, write each Chinese character according to its meaning.

#	CHARACTER	MEANING	DESCRIPTION & EXPLANATION
100		A household / door / family	Pictograph of a door leaf representing a household
101		Ten thousand / a great number	The ancient form is: 萬; the modern form has no direct connection with the meaning of its original form
102		Direction /square / upright / one side / place	Pictograph of a man giving directions
103		House / room	Pictograph of a household (character #100) and a place (character #102)
104		Up / above	A symbol of something on top or pointing upwards
105		Down / below	The reverse of character #104; above

#	CHARACTER	MEANING	DESCRIPTION & EXPLANATION
106		Card / to stop / to block	Pictograph of a device used to stop something from going up (character #104) or down (character #105), representing a card
107		Straight / vertical / frank / to straighten	Ten (character #4), eyes (character #33) looking at something, suggesting straight, direct
108		Tool / ability / to possess	Pictograph representing a tool
109		Really / truly / indeed / real / true / genuine	The early pictograph suggests something that has been unveiled, suggesting reality
110		A unit of length / inch / thumb	Pictograph a hand with a tool, representing a measure or an unit
111		Right / pair / to be opposite / to face / versus / for / vertical	Hand (character #77) and measure (character #110), suggesting "right" (t: 對)
112		Experience action marker / to cross / to go over / to pass (time)	Movement radical 辶 and measure (character #110), suggesting time (t: 過)
113		O'clock / time / when / hour / period	Day of the month (character #37) and measure (character #110), suggesting time (t: 時)

#	CHARACTER	MEANING	DESCRIPTION & EXPLANATION
114		Village	Wood (character #28) with 寸 phonetic (phonetics will be discussed later)
115		Tree	Wood (character #28) and vertical (character #111) (t: 樹)
116		Shellfish / currency	Pictograph of a shell (t: 貝)
117		To see / to meet / to appear	An eye 目 (character #33) on top of a person 儿; (t: 見)
118		Expensive / noble	Pictograph of a basket of money (shells) (t: 貴)
119		Appear / present / existing / current	Jade 玉 that can be seen (character #117) (t: 現)
120		Standing, upright	Person standing in upright position on the ground
121		To give birth / to reproduce / to produce / product	The traditional form 產 suggested birth with 厂 phonetic (phonetics will be discussed later)
122		Position / location / place / seat	A person (character #5) standing in assigned position (character #120)

#	CHARACTER	MEANING	DESCRIPTION & EXPLANATION
123		Station / to stand / to halt / to stop	Stand with 占 (character #17) phonetic (phonetics will be discussed later)
124		Small / tiny / few / young	An object broken into two small bits
125		Few / little / lack; young	Take away from already small (character #124)
126		Point (of needle) / sharp / pointed	Small 小 (character #124) and big 大 (character #7)
127		Dusk / evening	Pictograph of a crescent moon
128		Many / much / a lot of	Many moons (character #127)
129		Name / noun / famous	Identify in the dark (evening, character #127), suggesting name
130		Sentence / clause / phrase	Pictograph suggesting words from a mouth (character #45) that form a sentence

LESSON SIX: TEST 2

In the table below, without looking at what we have just studied, write the meaning of each Chinese character.

#	CHARACTER	MEANING	DESCRIPTION & EXPLANATION
100	户		Pictograph of a door leaf representing a household
101	万		The ancient form is: 萬; the modern form has no direct connection with the meaning of its original form
102	方		Pictograph of a man giving directions
103	房		Pictograph of a household (character #100) and a place (character #102)
104	上		A symbol of something on top or pointing upwards
105	下		The reverse of character #104; above
106	卡		Pictograph of a device used to stop something from going up (character #104) or down (character #105), representing a card
107	直		Ten (character #4), eyes (character #33) looking at something, suggesting straight, direct
108	具		Pictograph representing a tool

#	CHARACTER	MEANING	DESCRIPTION & EXPLANATION
109	真		The early pictograph suggests something that has been unveiled, suggesting reality
110	寸		Pictograph a hand with a tool, representing a measure or an unit
111	对		Hand (character #77) and measure (character #110), suggesting "right" (t: 對)
112	过		Movement radical 辶 and measure (character #110), suggesting time (t: 過)
113	时		Day of the month (character #37) and measure (character #110), suggesting time (t: 時)
114	村		Wood (character #28) with 寸 phonetic (phonetics will be discussed later)
115	树		Wood (character #28) and vertical (character #111) (t: 樹)
116	贝		Pictograph of a shell (t: 貝)
117	见		An eye 目 (character #33) on top of a person 儿; (t: 見)
118	贵		Pictograph of a basket of money (shells) (t: 貴)

#	CHARACTER	MEANING	DESCRIPTION & EXPLANATION
119	现		Jade 玉 that can be seen (character #117) (t: 現)
120	立		Person standing in upright position on the ground
121	产		The traditional form 產 suggested birth with 厂 phonetic (phonetics will be discussed later)
122	位		A person (character #5) standing in assigned position (character #120)
123	站		Stand with 占 (character #17) phonetic (phonetics will be discussed later)
124	小		An object broken into two small bits
125	少		Take away from already small (character #124)
126	尖		Small 小 (character #124) and big 大 (character #7)
127	夕		Pictograph of a crescent moon
128	多		Many moons (character #127)
129	名		Identify in the dark (evening, character #127), suggesting name
130	句		Pictograph suggesting words from a mouth (character #45) that form a sentence

PRACTICAL CHINESE CORNER

Looking at the 2 + 1 highlighted characters, what is the product concerned in this news broadcast?

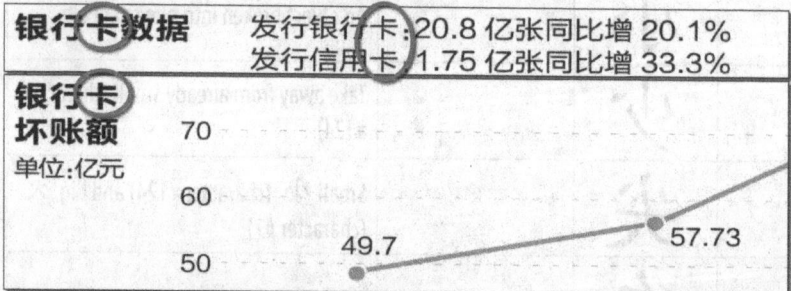

Looking at the highlighted character, what is the product concerned in this statistic report?

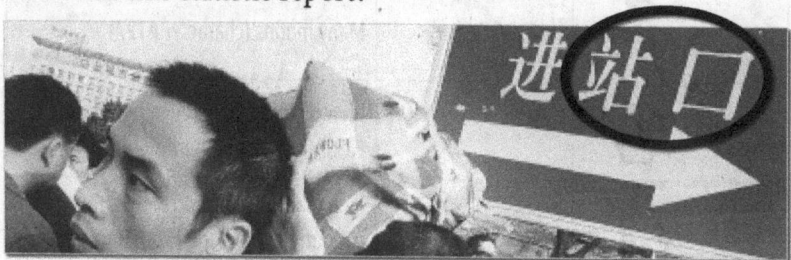

Looking at the highlighted characters, where was this picture taken?

LESSON SEVEN

七

Definition	Seven, each of seven seventh-day
Character Evolution	十 十 亏 七
Stroke Order	一 七
Chinese Proverb	七零八落

CHINESE IDIOMS

Chengyu 成语, literally "set phrases", are a type of traditional Chinese idiomatic expressions, most of which consist of four characters. Chengyu were widely used in Classical Chinese and are still common in Vernacular Chinese Writing and Spoken Chinese today. According to the most stringent definition, there are about 5,000 chengyu in the Chinese language, though some dictionaries list over 20,000.

Chengyu are mostly derived from ancient literature. The meaning of a chengyu usually surpasses the sum of the meanings carried by the four characters, as chengyu are often intimately linked with the myth, story or historical fact from which they were derived. As such, chengyu do not follow the usual grammatical structure and syntax of the modern Chinese spoken language, and are instead highly compact and rich in meaning.

The following three examples show that the meaning of the idiom can be totally different by only changing one character.

一 (yí) 日 (rì) 千 (qiān) 秋 (qiū): *"One day, a thousand autumns"*
Usage/Moral: *implies rapid changes; one day equals a thousand years*

一 (yí) 日 (rì) 千 (qiān) 里 (lǐ): *"One day, a thousand miles"*
Usage/Moral: *implies rapid progress; traveling a thousand miles in a day*

一 (yí) 日 (rì) 三 (sān) 秋 (qiū): *"One day, three autumns"*
Usage/Moral: *greatly missing someone; one day feels as long as three years*

LIST OF CHINESE CHARACTERS #131 - #156

The following list is a selection of characters that are very important to know in daily communication. Unlike the characters we have studied previously, some of them do not have an obvious connection to each other, but we advise you to study them very carefully, as they are as important as "I", "you", "to be", or "can", in English.

#	CHARACTER	ANCIENT FORM	MEANING	DESCRIPTION & EXPLANATION
131	不		(Negative prefix) / not / no	No short explanation available, but this character is important to know
132	还		Still / yet / in addition	No short explanation available, but this character is important to know (t: 還)
133	看		To see / to look at / to visit / it depends / to think	A hand shading the eye (character #33); to look, to see
134	会		To be able to / can / be likely to / to meet	No short explanation available, but this character is important to know
135	我		I / me / my	Pictograph of a hand holding a spear
136	你		You	A person (character #5) with 尔 phonetic (phonetics will be discussed later)
137	也		Also / too	No short explanation available, but this character is important to know

#	CHARACTER	ANCIENT FORM	MEANING	DESCRIPTION & EXPLANATION
138	地	埅	Earth / ground / field / place; -ly (adjective)	Soil (character #13) with 也 phonetic (phonetics will be discussed later)
139	他	伖	He / him	A person (character #5) with 也 phonetic (phonetics will be discussed later)
140	她	𤯔	She / her	A woman (character #53) with 也 phonetic (phonetics will be discussed later)
141	它	𧕦	It (used for animals or things) / its	A pictograph of a snake
142	东	🌲	East / host / landlord	The traditional version is 東; sun rising behind tree
143	南	峀	South	A pictograph of an ancient musical instrument
144	西	⊕	West	Pictograph of a bird roosting, suggesting sunset, therefore West
145	北	竹	North	Pictograph representing two persons back to back
146	要	燮	To want / will / going to/ must	Pictograph of two hands holding a woman, suggesting "wanting"
147	前	肖	Before / in front / ago / former / previous	Pictograph representing a forward movement, suggesting the front of something

#	CHARACTER	ANCIENT FORM	MEANING	DESCRIPTION & EXPLANATION
148	后	后	Back / behind / afterwards / after / later	A person (character #5) leaning forward to mouth (character #45) orders (t: 後)
149	左	左	Left	Hand (character #77) helping with the work; suggesting left hand
150	右	右	Right	Hand (character #77) working with mouth; suggesting right hand
151	中	中	Center / central / middle	An arrow going through the center of a target; 口 is not representing a mouth or frontier
152	很	很	Quite / very / awfully	Pictograph suggesting a fast movement with 艮 phonetic (phonetics will be discussed later)
153	春	春	Spring	Sun encouraging plants to shoot up
154	夏	夏	Summer	No short explanation available
155	秋	秋	Autumn	Wheat stalks burnt after the harvest in autumn
156	冬	冬	Winter	Pictograph representing the cold 冫 (see character #86); end of the year

Table 8: List of Chinese characters #131 - #156

LESSON SEVEN: STROKE ORDER & PRACTICE

The table below shows the order and direction of the strokes for each of the characters presented in this lesson. Now it's your turn to practice.

不	一	フ	不	不				
还	不	还						
看	一	二	三	手	看			
会	人	个	合	会	会			
我	一	二	于	手	托	我	我	
你	亻	仃	伫	你				
也	乛	也	也					
地	土	地						
他	亻	他						
她	女	她						
它	宀	宀	它					
东	一	七	车	东	东			
南	十	市	市	甬	甬	南		
西	一	冂	丙	西	西			
北	丨	十	北	北	北			
要	覀	要						

前	丶	⺍	芀	首	前	前			
后	一	厂	尸	后					
左	ナ	𠂇	左	左					
右	ナ	右							
中	口	中							
很	彳	彳	彳	彳	佷	很			
春	二	声	夫	春					
夏	百	頁	夏						
秋	禾	禾	秒	秒	秋				
冬	丿	夂	冬	冬					

LESSON SEVEN: TEST 1

In the table below, without looking at what we have just studied, write each Chinese character according to its meaning.

#	CHARACTER	MEANING	DESCRIPTION & EXPLANATION
131		(Negative prefix) / not / no	No short explanation available, but this character is important to know
132		Still / yet / in addition	No short explanation available, but this character is important to know (t: 還)

#	CHARACTER	MEANING	DESCRIPTION & EXPLANATION
133		To see / to look at/ to visit / it depends / to think	A hand shading the eye (character #33); to look, to see
134		To be able to / can / be likely to / to meet	No short explanation available, but this character is important to know
135		I / me / my	Pictograph of a hand holding a spear
136		You	A person (character #5) with 尔 phonetic (phonetics will be discussed later)
137		Also / too	No short explanation available, but this character is important to know
138		Earth / ground / field / place; -ly (adjective)	Soil (character #13) with 也 phonetic (phonetics will be discussed later)
139		He / him	A person (character #5) with 也 phonetic (phonetics will be discussed later)
140		She / her	A woman (character #53) with 也 phonetic (phonetics will be discussed later)
141		It (used for animals or things) / its	A pictograph of a snake

#	CHARACTER	MEANING	DESCRIPTION & EXPLANATION
142		East / host / landlord	The traditional version is 東; sun rising behind tree
143		South	A pictograph of an ancient musical instrument
144		West	Pictograph of a bird roosting, suggesting sunset, therefore West
145		North	Pictograph representing two persons back to back
146		To want / will / going to/ must	Pictograph of two hands holding a woman, suggesting "wanting"
147		Before / in front / ago / former / previous	Pictograph representing a forward movement, suggesting the front of something
148		Back / behind afterwards / after / later	A person (character #5) leaning forward to mouth (character #45) orders (t: 後)
149		Left	Hand (character #77) helping with the work; suggesting left hand
150		Right	Hand (character #77) working with mouth; suggesting right hand

#	CHARACTER	MEANING	DESCRIPTION & EXPLANATION
151		Center / central / middle	An arrow going through the center of a target; 口 is not representing a mouth or frontier
152		Quite / very / awfully	Pictograph suggesting a fast movement with 艮 phonetic (phonetics will be discussed later)
153		Spring	Sun encouraging plants to shoot up
154		Summer	No short explanation available
155		Autumn	Wheat stalks burnt after the harvest in autumn
156		Winter	Pictograph representing the cold 冫 (see character #86); end of the year

LESSON SEVEN: TEST 2

In the table below, without looking at what we have just studied, write the meaning of each Chinese character.

#	CHARACTER	MEANING	DESCRIPTION & EXPLANATION
131	不		No short explanation available, but this character is important to know

#	CHARACTER	MEANING	DESCRIPTION & EXPLANATION
132	还		No short explanation available, but this character is important to know (t: 還)
133	看		A hand shading the eye (character #33); to look, to see
134	会		No short explanation available, but this character is important to know
135	我		Pictograph of a hand holding a spear
136	你		A person (character #5) with 尔 phonetic (phonetics will be discussed later)
137	也		No short explanation available, but this character is important to know
138	地		Soil (character #13) with 也 phonetic (phonetics will be discussed later)
139	他		A person (character #5) with 也 phonetic (phonetics will be discussed later)
140	她		A woman (character #53) with 也 phonetic (phonetics will be discussed later)
141	它		A pictograph of a snake

#	CHARACTER	MEANING	DESCRIPTION & EXPLANATION
142	东		The traditional version is 東; sun rising behind tree
143	南		A pictograph of an ancient musical instrument
144	西		Pictograph of a bird roosting, suggesting sunset, therefore West
145	北		Pictograph representing two persons back to back
146	要		Pictograph of two hands holding a woman, suggesting "wanting"
147	前		Pictograph representing a forward movement, suggesting the front of something
148	后		A person (character #5) leaning forward to mouth (character #45) orders (t: 後)
149	左		Hand (character #77) helping with the work; suggesting left hand
150	右		Hand (character #77) working with mouth; suggesting right hand
151	中		An arrow going through the center of a target; 口 is not representing a mouth or frontier

#	CHARACTER	MEANING	DESCRIPTION & EXPLANATION
152	很		Pictograph suggesting a fast movement with 艮 phonetic (phonetics will be discussed later)
153	春		Sun encouraging plants to shoot up
154	夏		No short explanation available
155	秋		Wheat stalks burnt after the harvest in autumn
156	冬		Pictograph representing the cold 冫 (see character #86); end of the year

PRACTICAL CHINESE CORNER

According to the 2 circled characters, the picture above is about "getting/returning home." What are the 4 highlighted characters trying to tell us?

This advertisement is about the difficulty of buying train tickets at a certain time of the year. When season or time of the year is it?

LESSON EIGHT

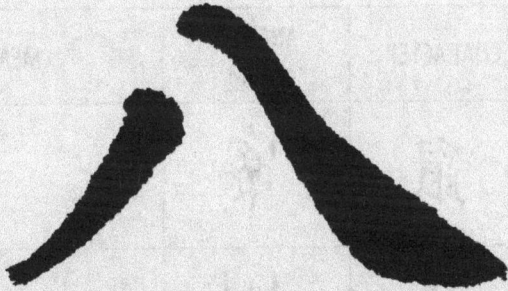

Definition	Eight
Character Evolution	
Stroke Order	丿　八
Chinese Proverb	八而威风

THE CHINESE ZODIAC AND THE USE OF "ANIMAL" RADICAL

In lesson two, section "Radicals" on page 26, we learned about Chinese radicals, which is a particularly important part of the Chinese writing system to understand. In this lesson, we will deepen this knowledge, through the analysis of the 12 Chinese animals that form the Chinese Zodiac.

#	CHARACTER	ANCIENT FORM	MEANING
157	鼠		Rat
158	牛		Ox
159	虎		Tiger
160	兔		Rabbit
161	龙		Dragon (t: 龍)
162	蛇		Snake

#	CHARACTER	ANCIENT FORM	MEANING
163	马	象	Horse (t: 馬)
164	羊	￥	Sheep
165	猴	猴	Monkey
166	鸡	雞	Fowl (Chicken) (t: 雞)
167	狗	狗	Dog
168	猪	豬	Pig (t: 豬)

Table 9: List of Chinese characters #157 - #168

Three of the twelve animals should be familiar to you: 马 (t: 馬, horse), 牛 (ox) and 羊 (sheep). But we shall use all twelve of them to illustrate and review the principle of classifying a character according to its radical. We have already considered this principle in the case of the "wood" radical (木), which indicates that the combination in which it is incorporated, has something to do with trees, wood, construction and so on. But the "animal" radical (犭) is even more helpful than the "wood" radical. Our dictionary lists more than a hundred characters under the "animal" radical, and almost all of them represent some species of animal, whereas the "wood" radical has twice as many characters, and by no means are all characters directly connected with wood.

The "fish" radical (t: 鱼) is particularly helpful. Most of the characters listed under this radical are the names of some sort of fish. One exception is 鳄, which means crocodile. This presents us with a combination consisting of the "fish" radical on the left, indicating that the character we are looking at represents some sort of an aquatic animal, and a line drawing of a beast with two squares at the top to represent the idea of the heavy scales covering its body.

Whenever we see the "fish" radical, we are probably looking at the name of a fish, although we may not know its name in English, and still less in Chinese. There are obviously many species of fish; among them in our dictionary are a sting-ray and a left-eyed flounder.

The combinations representing 猪 (t: 豬, pig), 猴 (monkey) and 狗 (dog) all use our "animal"radical (犭) to indicate that they are in the "animal" category. For the present, we will ignore the elements on the right hand side, which have been borrowed to indicate sound, not meaning. We shall explain the idea of phonetic borrowing later.

Other signs of the Zodiac confirm how useful our "animal" radicals can be:

$$ 鸟 \Rightarrow 鸡 $$

鸡 (t: 雞), means "chicken". It uses the "bird" radical (鸟). Most of the characters with this radical have a connection with some bird species.

$$ 虫 \Rightarrow 蛇 $$

蛇 (snake) uses the 虫 radical, which indicates a wide range of animal life, such as frogs, snakes, insects and butterflies. Under this radical, about half are animals of some sort. We can, for convenience call it the "insect" radical, although it covers a range well outside the normal English meaning of "insect". We have given it a section in the Appendices to illustrate the theme that the radicals are often, but not always, useful memory aids.

The other Zodiac animals which we have not yet studied are "rat", "tiger", "rabbit" and "dragon."

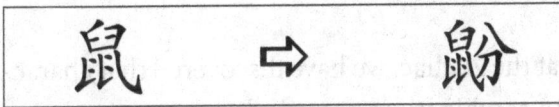

鼠 ⇨ 鼢

鼠 means rat or a mouse, 鼢 is a variety of mole. 鼠 was originally a sketch of an animal, showing head, whiskers, teeth and tail.

虍 ⇨ 虎

虍 means the stripes of a tiger, 虎 means a tiger. 虎 was originally a straightforward line sketch of a striped animal.

刀 ⇨ 兔

兔 is a sketch of such an animal crouching, alert to danger. There are several characters under this radical.

Few of them are directly connected to animals. 冤 means injustice, it suggests a caged rabbit. Most of them have been borrowed for sound, not for meaning.

龙 (t: 龍) is a radical and also a character. It means "dragon", which is one of the most commonly used words in the Chinese lexicon. It has, during more than three thousand years, become almost totally divorced from its original pictographic form. Under this radical, few of the characters have a meaning related to "dragon", it is used mostly for phonetic purposes.

Thus far, looking at the Zodiac, we have discovered that characters are often used in combination, not to indicate meaning but to suggest a sound. We have voluntarily avoided any discussion on the relevance of sound, but we shall look in the next lesson at the role of sound in the construction of characters. Clearly, sound is of little relevance to beginners, not yet conversant with the sounds of the Chinese language.

LESSON EIGHT: STROKE ORDER & PRACTICE

The table below shows the order and direction of the strokes for each of the characters presented in this lesson. Now it's your turn to practice.

鼠	厂	冖	冃	臼	臼	臼	鼠	鼠		
牛	ノ	乇	牛							
虎	𠂉	龶	广	虍	虖	虎				
兔	ノ	𠂉	甹	弇	兔	兔				

龙	亠	龙	龙					
蛇	中	虫	虫	蛇				
马	⁊	马	马					
羊	丶	丷	兰	羊				
猴	✓	犭	犭	犭	犭	犷	犷	猴
鸡	又	又	邓	邓	鸡	鸡		
狗	犭	狗						
猪	犭	犷	犷	猪				

LESSON EIGHT: TEST 1

In the table below, we have selected characters we have not studied yet, do not be frightened. According to the "Table 2: Example of common radicals" on page 29 and "Table 9: List of Chinese characters #157 - #168" on page 102, write down the radical of each characters and select the correct radical category.

Keep in mind that a radical does not always give a clue to the real meaning of the character. See "Test Answer Key 2" on page 172 for answers.

#	RADICAL	MEANING		EXAMPLE
1		☐ Wood ☐ Animal		犸
2		☐ Water ☐ Language		讯

#	RADICAL	MEANING	EXAMPLE
3		☐ Animal ☐ Root	羚
4		☐ Fish ☐ Language	鲐
5		☐ Plant ☐ House	花
6		☐ Animal ☐ Hair	彪
7		☐ Tree ☐ Animal	驼
8		☐ Sickness ☐ Weather	病
9		☐ Eye ☐ Food	盲
10		☐ Animal ☐ Cloth	狍
11		☐ Animal ☐ Flower	牡
12		☐ Field ☐ Ice	男
13		☐ Roof ☐ Musical instrument	官
14		☐ Liquid ☐ Door	闯
15		☐ Roof ☐ Dancer	家

PRACTICAL CHINESE CORNER

Write under each Chinese character the name of the animal it represents.

鼠	龙	猴	兔
牛	蛇	鸡	羊
虎	马	狗	猪

According to the character highlighted above, in the Chinese Zodiac what animal represents the year 2010?

LESSON NINE

九

Definition	Nine, many, numerous
Character Evolution	𢀓 ﻉ 九 九
Stroke Order	丿 九
Chinese Proverb	九牛一毛

DIALECTS, SOUNDS, SPELLING AND BORROWINGS FOR PHONETIC REASONS

INTRODUCTION

Putong Hua 普通话, the modern spoken language based on the Beijing dialect, is now used throughout the whole of China. However until recently, it was not spoken throughout China. The written language, known only to a minority: scholars, officials; the "literati", performed the same function in the Chinese Empire as Latin did for the Roman Empire. This allowed every educated man to communicate throughout the Empire, regardless of their mother tongue.

More than eighty "Dialects" were listed in the Chinese Statistical record in the 1990's. As a Cantonese student in 1947, we soon found that Cantonese was useless outside Guangdong Province: we could only communicate in writing. The Chinese government, understandably, has promoted the use of Putong Hua, and local "dialects" are being less used.

The so-called "dialects", such as Cantonese, Hakka, Hokkien, Teochew, Shanghainese, and Hainanese of the south, are as different from each other as are Italian, French and Spanish or English and German. These "dialects" share roots but are not understood by a person from a different province, nor do they have any officially agreed written form.

Non-Chinese often find it difficult to conceive of a written language which is not based on any form of alphabet. The table below illustrates how different the sounds of the "dialects" can be. We have used idiosyncratic spellings in the Mandarin and Cantonese columns to help English speakers to imagine the sounds easily.

#	CHARACTER	PINYIN	MANDARIN	CANTONESE
1	一	yī	yee	yat
2	二	èr	er	yee
3	三	sān	san	saam
4	四	sì	szi	say
5	五	wǔ	woo	ng
6	六	liù	liu	luk
7	七	qī	chee	chut
8	八	bā	ba	baat
9	九	jiǔ	jiu	gau
10	十	shí	sher	sup

Table 10: Pronunciation in Pinyin, Mandarin, and Cantonese

Until Mandarin, now Putong Hua, became a nationwide language, people from two different provinces could only communicate easily if both knew the written language.

DISCUSSION

Until the beginning of the 20th century, all who could read could understand something of the Chinese classics. It was as if all who knew modern English could still read Beowulf, Chaucer and Shakespeare with ease, despite the many centuries that had passed. But the Chinese written language 文言 (Wenyan), was a pithy, concise, scholar's language and difficult to learn, so the general public were excluded. It was, therefore, natural that reformers should seek to simplify the literary written language. After the revolution of 1911, Chinese intellectuals introduced a new style of Chinese writing which would be more accessible to the masses. The new style was called 白话 (bai hua, literally "white speech", the language of the people) and newspapers, novels, and plays became more accessible. But in the process, it made the ancient classics become something of a foreign language. It was perhaps in some ways analogous to what took place in Britain. In the 19th century, every educated person could read Latin and writers assumed that they could freely use Latin quotations, without needing to supply their readers with a translation. In the 21st century, no writer would make that assumption. The Chinese written language reformers have produced a similar effect: few can read the classics with ease.

A Chinese commission was established in the 1950's to find a standard formula for transliterating the national language (Putong Hua) into roman letters. Pinyin (literally the putting together of sounds) has been a success. But like any "romanization", it cannot provide an effective substitute for Chinese characters because, as we will see in the next lesson, there are so many words in Chinese which sound the same. The traditional form of Chinese writing overcame the homophone problems: 人 (a person) does not look the same as 仁 (benevolence) but in Pinyin both are romanized as "ren" (rén). Of course to a limited extent, this problem exists in English. A bowl can be a dish, an amphitheater, or the ball used in the game of bowls. But usually different words are spelled differently. "Knight" and "night" certainly do not look the same. The number of homophones in the Chinese language is much greater, as a glance at any Chinese-English dictionary will confirm. The Unihan database (see "Further reading" on page 138) shows 448 Chinese characters grouped under the pinyin heading "ji". This is a formidable number of homophones. There are 126 words listed under "ji" first tone (jī) (for information on tones, see "The function of sound in the Chinese written language" on page 115), 143 under "ji" second tone (jí), 44 under "ji" third tone (jǐ), and 162 under "ji" fourth tone (jì). They range through small table (几), beat (击), machine (机), chicken (鸡), impatient (急), etc. Of course context helps, and fortunately two words are usually put together thus, in effect, making a two syllable word.

PRACTICAL CHINESE CORNER

In the table below, write in Chinese characters the name of each
of the 4 seasons.

Write in Chinese characters the name of the four cardinal direc-
tions, north, south, east, and west.

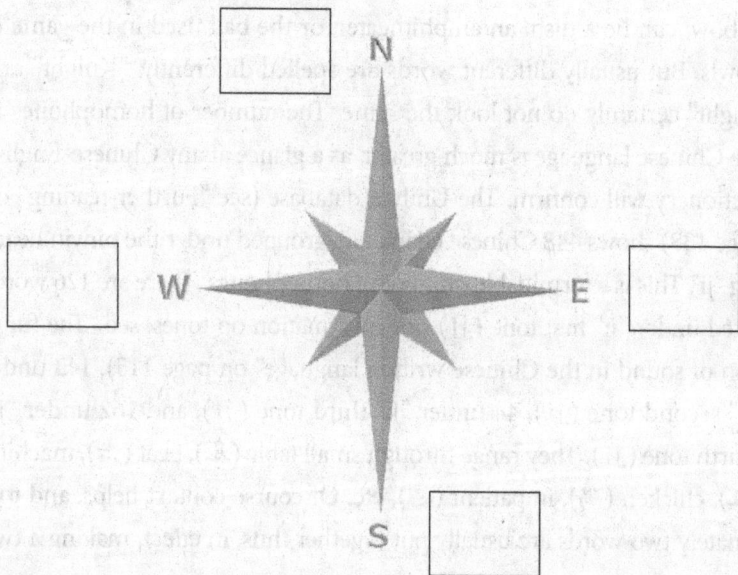

十

Definition	Ten, complete
Character Evolution	丨 ❙ 十 十
Stroke Order	一 十				
Chinese Proverb	十全十美

THE FUNCTION OF SOUND IN THE CHINESE WRITTEN LANGUAGE

We have put this subject towards the end because our concern has been with the appearance of Chinese characters, the elements which make it up and the meaning. Even if we already knew something of the spoken language and its sounds, it would not have helped us to analyze, and understand Chinese characters under study; at worst it would have confused us. But now the time has come to introduce "sound", as an important element in the make-up of Chinese characters.

As we have discussed in the previous lesson, until the late 20th Century, oral communication was hardly possible between the inhabitants of the North and South. Their mother tongues were mutually incomprehensible, and all their so called "dialects", as different as French and English, were incomprehensible to a Mandarin speaker. The only effective means of communication was the written language.

The differences in pronunciation of surnames give a good illustration of the differences between the so called "dialects". A Mr. Wu, from Beijing would find that Wu (吴) was pronounced Goh in Fujian, and Ng in Guangdong. Mr. Chen (陈) from Beijing would find his name pronounced as Tan in Xiamen and Chan in Guangzhou.

So until very recently, the written language was all-important as the only means of communicating across the length and breadth of China; but its importance as a nationwide means of communication had nothing to do with the sounds allotted to the Chinese characters by Mandarin speakers. It functioned as a national written language, because readers did not need to know how it was pronounced in Beijing, they simply needed to know what it meant. None of the linguistic reforms introduced since 1949 have altered the basics of the Wenyan (文言), the Classical Language. For eminently sensible and practical reasons, the Chinese characters remain. They overcome the problems of a language with relatively few spoken syllables, and a great number of words which are spelled the same way in Pinyin, although they look very different when written in the traditional Chinese script, as we have seen in previous lessons.

In this book, the word "sound" has hardly been mentioned. But we have noticed in passing that sometimes a Chinese character has been used as an element in a combination to suggest sound, not to indicate meaning. This device is used frequently.

THE TONE SYSTEM

The tone systems in Western languages are arbitrary and personal. Nevertheless everyone uses tones when speaking English. Some examples are:

- Really?　↗　　Question
- Really　　→　　Neutral observation
- Really　　↘　　Exasperation

We certainly do use "tones" in Western language. But the "tones" are not permanently attached to a word: they are related to mood, context, emphasis, rhetoric, and the circumstances.

Chinese is not the only language which attaches "tones" permanently to a word, but it is the most important. Mandarin has four tones (plus one neutral tone), and Cantonese has nine tones. But whether we look at four or nine, we are looking at something alien to any Western language. It probably matters little if you get the tones wrong counting from one to ten: you can write in "Arabic Numbers", use a pocket calculator, or even use fingers. But it can matter a great deal in other circumstances.

The figure below illustrates the 4 tones of the Chinese Mandarin language:

PITCH

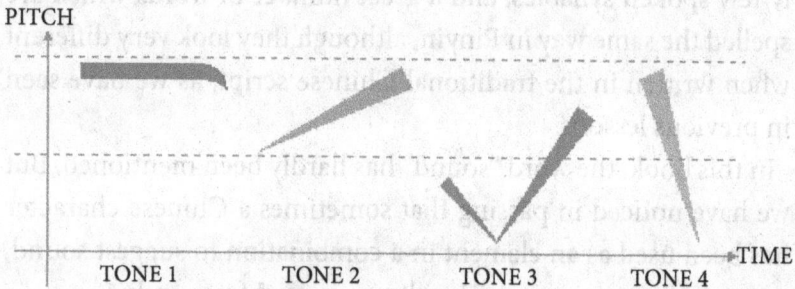

TONE 1   TONE 2   TONE 3   TONE 4   TIME

Take the monosyllable "ma" for example:

- mā, 妈, Mother, 1st tone
- má, 麻, Hemp, 2nd tone
- mǎ, 马, Horse, 3rd tone
- mà, 骂, Curse, 4th tone
- ma, 吗, Interrogative particle, neutral tone

There could be plenty of room for confusion, consternation, or amusement using the wrong tone. Or take the entry "ji" with first tone, (jī). In the Unihan Database under which there are more than a hundred characters, each has a different appearance and a different meaning, but all are written exactly the same way in Pinyin.

Clearly, it is worth investing time in mastering the tones. Sadly, there are very few foreigners who fully master the tones in the sense that every word they learn is welded permanently in their brain to its tone. The reasons for this sad state of affairs are not hard to find. Firstly, most foreigners, impatient to start communicating immediately, will probably not be willing to spend hours reciting "tone tables". Secondly, university teachers will not use such basic teaching techniques. Chanting "Tone Tables" is not likely to figure high in their priorities, so their students move swiftly on to attempts at communication without perfecting their tones.

When we started to learn Chinese, every morning for six days a week, we started with over an hour of "chanting": the teacher read characters, and we copied the sound, reading the romanized version. Every day for a month we always started with "chanting" sessions. It worked. This tone drill method is not often used in institutes of learning. The students know the theory but not the practice.

It is a pity that few foreigners master their "tones" at the very beginning of their studies. Getting the tones right is not an intellectual exercise but an exercise in imitation.

In the following table, we have given the meaning, Pinyin and tone for each of the characters we have studied thus far. It is important to note that some characters have more than one Pinyin or tone. In order not to complicate this lesson, the most commonly used Pinyin is given. For more information, the student will have to refer to a dictionary.

Our main goal throughout this book is not to focus on the sound of characters, but to provide an easy and efficient way to learn and remember their meaning according to their structure.

The following table will provide you a first step towards learning the sound of Chinese Mandarin[1].

(1) A particularly good resource to learn how to pronounce Pinyin sounds is: http://www.quickmandarin.com/chinesepinyintable/

#	CHAR	PINYIN	DEFINITION	#	CHAR	PINYIN	DEFINITION
1	一	yī	One	15	广	guǎng	Wide
2	二	èr	Two	16	座	zuò	Seat
3	三	sān	Three	17	占	zhàn	To occupy
4	十	shí	Ten	18	点	diǎn	A little
5	人	rén	Person	19	店	diàn	Shop
6	个	gè	Individual	20	床	chuáng	Bed
7	大	dà	Big	21	去	qù	To go
8	太	tài	Too	22	在	zài	Located at
9	天	tiān	Sky, day	23	王	wáng	King
10	从	cóng	To follow	24	主	zhǔ	Master
11	内	nèi	Inside	25	住	zhù	To live
12	肉	ròu	Meat	26	国	guó	Country
13	土	tǔ	Earth	27	因	yīn	Cause
14	坐	zuò	To sit	28	木	mù	Tree

#	CHAR	PINYIN	DEFINITION	#	CHAR	PINYIN	DEFINITION
29	林	lín	Forest	43	早	zǎo	Early
30	森	sēn	Dense forest	44	昨	zuó	Yesterday
31	休	xiū	To rest	45	口	kǒu	Mouth
32	本	běn	Root	46	喝	hē	To drink
33	目	mù	Eye	47	禾	hé	Millet
34	相	xiāng	Appearance	48	和	hé	And
35	心	xīn	Heart	49	香	xiāng	Fragrant
36	想	xiǎng	To think	50	吃	chī	To eat
37	日	rì	Sun, day	51	品	pǐn	Article
38	白	bái	White	52	回	huí	To go back
39	勺	sháo	Spoon	53	女	nǚ	Woman
40	的	de	Of	54	了	le	Tense indicator
41	百	bǎi	Hundred	55	子	zǐ	Son / Small
42	是	shì	To be	56	好	hǎo	Good

#	CHAR	PINYIN	DEFINITION	#	CHAR	PINYIN	DEFINITION
57	安	ān	Peace	71	门	mén	Door
58	字	zì	Letter	72	们	men	Plural suffix
59	家	jiā	Home	73	问	wèn	To ask
60	妈	mā	Mother	74	间	jiān	Between
61	吗	ma	Question mark	75	买	mǎi	To buy
62	骂	mà	To scold	76	卖	mài	To sell
63	石	shí	Rock	77	又	yòu	Once again
64	码	mǎ	Number	78	双	shuāng	A pair
65	田	tián	Field	79	友	yǒu	Friend
66	力	lì	Strength	80	没	méi	Negative prefix
67	办	bàn	To do	81	刀	dāo	Knife
68	为	wèi	Because of	82	米	mǐ	Rice
69	男	nán	Male	83	来	lái	To come
70	果	guǒ	Fruit	84	粉	fěn	Powder

#	CHAR	PINYIN	DEFINITION	#	CHAR	PINYIN	DEFINITION
85	水	shuǐ	Water	99	冷	lěng	Cold
86	冰	bīng	Ice	100	户	hù	Household
87	汁	zhī	Juice	101	万	wàn	Ten thousand
88	千	qiān	Thousand	102	方	fāng	Direction
89	开	kāi	To open	103	房	fáng	House
90	古	gǔ	Ancient	104	上	shàng	Up
91	舌	shé	Tongue	105	下	xià	Down
92	话	huà	Language	106	卡	kǎ	Card
93	活	huó	To live	107	直	zhí	Straight
94	月	yuè	Month	108	具	jù	Tool
95	朋	péng	Friend	109	真	zhēn	Really
96	明	míng	Clear	110	寸	cùn	Unit of length
97	有	yǒu	To have	111	对	duì	Right
98	今	jīn	Today	112	过	guò	Experience marker

#	CHAR	PINYIN	DEFINITION	#	CHAR	PINYIN	DEFINITION
113	时	shí	O'clock	127	夕	xī	Dusk
114	村	cūn	Village	128	多	duō	Many
115	树	shù	Tree	129	名	míng	Name
116	贝	bèi	Shell	130	句	jù	Sentence
117	见	jiàn	To see	131	不	bù	Negative prefix
118	贵	guì	Expensive	132	还	hái	Still, yet
119	现	xiàn	Appear	133	看	kàn	To see
120	立	lì	Standing	134	会	huì	Can
121	产	chǎn	To give birth	135	我	wǒ	I
122	位	wèi	Position	136	你	nǐ	You
123	站	zhàn	Station	137	也	yě	And
124	小	xiǎo	Small	138	地	dì	Ground
125	少	shǎo	Few	139	他	tā	He
126	尖	jiān	Point, sharp	140	她	tā	She

#	CHAR	PINYIN	DEFINITION	#	CHAR	PINYIN	DEFINITION
141	它	tā	It	155	秋	qiū	Autumn
142	东	dōng	East	156	冬	dōng	Winter
143	南	nán	South	157	鼠	shǔ	Rat
144	西	xī	West	158	牛	niú	Ox
145	北	běi	North	159	虎	hǔ	Tiger
146	要	yào	To have	160	兔	tù	Rabbit
147	前	qián	Before, front	161	龙	lóng	Dragon
148	后	hòu	After, back	162	蛇	shé	Snake
149	左	zuǒ	Left	163	马	mǎ	Horse
150	右	yòu	Right	164	羊	yáng	Sheep
151	中	zhōng	Center	165	猴	hóu	Monkey
152	很	hěn	Very	166	鸡	jī	Fowl (Chicken)
153	春	chūn	Spring	167	狗	gǒu	Dog
154	夏	xià	Summer	168	猪	zhū	Pig

Table 11: Pinyin sounds of our selection of 168 Chinese characters

DO CHARACTERS WITH SIMILAR RADICALS OR STRUCTURE HAVE SIMILAR SOUND AND/OR MEANING?

This section is an appendix to the present lesson. If you feel that it will confuse you, go to the next chapter and the final tests.

We have already seen in lesson 9, "Discussion" on page 111, that for a given "Pinyin" sound, there can be more than one character associated. The following question we will look at is: "do characters with similar radicals or structure have similar sound and or meaning?" The answer is "not always."

The table below uses the radical 虫, conventionally known as the insect radical, to demonstrate that the phonetic principle is used as often, if not more often, than the pictorial principle, in the construction of Chinese characters. The list also provides a useful demonstration of the problems of homophones. Here we have 5 Chinese characters, all having the same radical, but with different sounds in Pinyin.

#	CHARACTER	MEANING	PINYIN
1	虫	Insect; worm	chóng
2	虱	Louse	shī
3	虾	Shrimp	xiā
4	虽	Although; even though	suī

#	CHARACTER	MEANING	PINYIN
5	蚊	Mosquito	wén

Table 12: Example of Pinyin sounds for the radical 虫

If we extend this table to 30 characters under the same radical 虫, we will see that:

- 19 characters have the names of animals ranging from louse to snake.
- 4 characters are animal products, eggs, honey, bees and wax.
- 4 characters are verbs related to the movements of worms and snakes.
- 3 characters are not related to the animal world.

So the 虫 radical provides a clue to meaning for 27 out of the 30 characters under the 虫 radical in the dictionary.

Many may wonder why the most enthusiastic Chinese reformers have not acted to abolish Chinese characters, and replace them with Pinyin. The question is easily answered by reference to the many words grouped under one Pinyin heading.

Now let us look at the way in which the scribes have used sound to expand their options when creating new Chinese characters. Let us be clear, when Chinese characters are borrowed for phonetic purposes, they do not give a precise indicator of the sound in the way that the letters of the alphabet do where "B" always sounds like the "B" in "ball", and "D" always sounds like the "D" in "dog". The characters borrowed for phonetic purposes only make a suggestion that the sound of the character will have some connection with the sound of the borrowed element.

We shall now proceed, on the good Chinese proverbial principle that one picture is worth ten thousand words, to provide examples of the borrowing of characters for the purpose of suggesting sound. If we are very lucky, we will face a combination which consists of a familiar character, used as a radical, to suggest category of meaning, and a familiar character used to suggest sound. Unfortunately the system is seldom so kind. But the phonetic principle helps memory, even if it is imprecise.

The four examples below have the same Pinyin and the same tone, but on this occasion each of them has ceased to be a guide to the meaning and become a guide to sound.

CHARACTER	MEANING OF COMBINATION	ELEMENTS OF COMBINATION	PINYIN
生	Give birth, bear, grow, Living	生 as the radical	shēng
笙	Small gourd-shaped musical instrument	竹 as the radical; 生 as the phonetic	shēng
甥	Sister's child	生 is the radical, also used as a phonetic	shēng
牲	Sacrificial animal	牜 as the radical; 生 as a phonetic	shēng

Table 13: Example of phonetic borrowings

Learning Chinese characters can be confusing for those in need of a systematic set of rules. We have seen throughout this lesson that it is not always the case. However, experience has taught us that the more characters you learn or memorize, the easier it becomes. If more than one billion people are able to use them daily to communicate, why not you? The best advice we can give you from now on is 加油 ("Jiāyóu", keep it up!)

PRACTICAL CHINESE CORNER

In the table below, write in Chinese characters the equivalent for I, My, She, He, etc.

	I My	
	He His	
	She Her	
	They (women) Theirs (women)	
	They (men) Theirs (men)	
	It (animal or thing) Its (animal or thing)	
	They (animals or things) Theirs (animals or things)	

PRACTICAL CHINESE

用

Definition	To use, employ, apply
Character Evolution	用　用　用　用
Stroke Order	丿　刀　月　月　用
Chinese Proverb	用心良苦

　　　Brian Stewart

YOUR FIRST STORY IN CHINESE

If you have been studying with us the characters introduced in the lessons 1 to 10, you should be able to read the following text. At first sight, it looks impossible. Don't panic, none of the characters that follow are new to you.

☞ First, see if you can grasp its meaning. It might be difficult, but try, one character after another.

　　我的名字是王冰。我是西方人，十一月七日来了中国。中国是一个好地方，东西很好吃，中国人也很友好。我住在西安。西安的小吃很有名，不过冬天太冷了，1°C左右。

　　我有一个日本朋友，他一直想来中国。昨天他和他的妈妈来西安看我。现在他们住在我家。

　　今天早上我们去吃东西时，人太多了。我们去点东西时，有人占了我们的座位。我们又去了人少一点的一家店。我的朋友点了羊肉粉，他的妈妈不吃牛羊肉，点了鸡肉粉。我们没有点喝的东西，因为太贵了。

　　我们明天要去买香水。有一家店的香水很好。因为还想回来买很多东西，我办了VIP卡。

　　我的男朋友住在广西，从来没有见过他们。因为他们十二月五日前还在中国，我的男朋友会从广西过来见他们。

　　我的日本朋友在中国很开心，他们还想来中国。

☞ Let's now translate each Chinese character:

我的名字是王冰。我是西方人，十一月七日来了中国。

中国是一个好地方，东西很好吃，中国人也很友好。

我住在西安。西安的小吃很有名，不过冬天太冷了，

1°C左右。

我有一个日本朋友，他一直想来中国。昨天他和他的

妈妈来西安看我。现在他们住在我家。

今天早上我们去吃东西时，人太多了。我们去点东西

时，有人占了我们的座位。我们又去了人少一点的一家

店。我的朋友点了羊肉粉，他的妈妈不吃牛羊肉，

点了鸡肉粉。我们没有点喝的东西，因为太贵了。

我们明天要去买香水。有一家店的香水很好。

因为还想回来买很多东西，我办了VIP卡。

我的男朋友住在广西，从来没有见过他们。因为他们十

二月五日前还在中国，我的男朋友会从广西过来见他们。

我的日本朋友在中国很开心，他们还想来中国。

☞ In the text above there are several 2-character words (in gray color), which we have not studied, but you should know each character that composes them. Here are the corresponding translations and explanations:

名字 : Name
王冰 : A person's surname
中国 : "Middle Kingdom"; China
地方 : "Ground-place"; place
友好 : "Friendly-friendly"; friendly
东西 : "East-West"; things (food, objects, etc.)
西安 : Xi'an, a City in China
冬天 : "Winter + day"; winter
左右 : "Left + right"; about
日本 : "Sun + root"; Japan
朋友 : "Friend + friend"; friend

一直 : "One-straight"; all along
昨天 : "Yesterday + day"; yesterday
坐位 : "Seat + location"; seat
香水 : "Fragrant + water"; perfume
广西 : Guangxi Province
从来 : "From + come"; never
开心 : "Open + heart"; happy

☞ Chinese to English translation:

My name is Wang Bing. I am a Westerner. On the 7th of November, I arrived in China. China is a great place, the food is very good, and Chinese people are very friendly. I live in Xi'an. Food (little street snacks) in Xi'an is very famous, but winter is too cold, about 1°C.

I have a Japanese friend. For a long time he has wanted to come to China. Yesterday, he and his mother arrived in Xi'an to see me. They now live in my house.

This morning we went to eat food, but there were too many people. While we were placing an order, some people took our seats, we then went to another less crowded restaurant. My friend ordered mutton noodle. His mother does not eat beef nor mutton, so she ordered chicken noodle. We didn't order drinks because it was too expensive.

Tomorrow we're going to buy perfume. There is a very good perfume shop around. Because we wanted to buy in large quantities, we got a VIP card.

My boyfriend lives in Guangxi, he has never met my friends. Because they will be in China until January 5th, my boyfriend will come from Guangxi to see them.

My friends had a good time in China, they are thinking of coming again.

☞ Below is the text in English, in its literal form. Your task is, without looking at the original text, to translate it into Chinese.

□□□□□□□。□□□□□, □□□□□□□□□□。

My / name / is / Wang / Bing. I am / Westerner. 11(th) / month / 7(th) / day / arrived / China.

□□□□□□□□□, □□□□□, □□□□□□□□。

China / is / one / good / place, things / very / good / to eat, Chinese / people / also / very / friendly.

□□□□□□。□□□□□□□□, □□□□□□□□,

I / live / in / Xi'an. Xi'an /of / small + eat (snacks) / very / has + name (famous), but / winter / too / cold,

1°C□□。

1°C / about.

□□□□□□□□, □□□□□□□□。□□□□□□□

I / have / a / Japan / friend, he / straight (from long) / wanted / to come to / China. Yesterday / he / and / his

□□□□□□□□。□□□□□□□□□。

mother / arrived / Xi'an / to see / me. Now / they /live / at / my / home.

□□□□□□□□□□□□□, □□□□□。□□□□□□

Today / morning / we / went / to eat / things / time (at the time of), people / too / many. We / went / to order / things

□, □□□□□□□□□。 □□□□□□□□□□

time , there were / people / occupied / our / seats. We / again / went /
people / less / one + little (little) / of

□□□。 □□□□□□□□□□, □□□□□□□□□,
one / home + shop (restaurant). My / friend / ordered / sheep / meat /
noodle, his / mother / does not / eat / beef / sheep / meat,

□□□□□□。 □□□□□□□□□, □□□□□□。
ordered / chicken / meat / noodle. We / did not / order / drink +
things (drinks), because / too / expensive.

□□□□□□□□□□。 □□□□□□□□□□。
We / tomorrow / want / to go / to buy / perfume. There is / a / house-
shop (shop) / of / perfume / very / good.

□□□□□□□□□□□, □□□VIP□。
Because / also / think / come back / to buy / a lot / things, we / did / VIP / card.

□□□□□□□□□, □□□□□□□□。 □□□□
My / boyfriend / lives / in / Guangxi, from + to come (never) /
did / meet /them. Because / they

□□□□□□□□□, □□□□□□□□□□□□。
12(th) month 5(th) day / before / still / in / China, my / boyfriend /
wants / from / Guangxi / come / to see / them.

□□□□□□□□□□□, □□□□□□。
My / Japan / friends / in / China / very / happy, they / still / think / to
come to / China.

THE HARDEST LANGUAGE IN THE WORLD?

There is no agreed means of ranking the languages of the world according to difficulty. Some languages are harder to pronounce, and some have more complex syntax, or grammar. Some use the Roman alphabet, while the Japanese use some characters. The Arabs use a sort of alphabet written in a flowing script; the Russians Cyrillic; the Grecians have the Greek alphabet, and all over Asia there are Sanskrit based scripts which are totally unintelligible to a newcomer.

There are hundreds of languages for which there was no written version, until missionaries arrived and had to invent a written form in order to produce Holy Books in the vernacular. In Vietnam and Fiji, to use examples of languages of which we have some knowledge, the missionaries, Roman Catholic French in the one case, and Scottish Presbyterian in the other, produced some idiosyncratic solutions, but their efforts have stood the test of time.

Chinese, probably the most widely used language in the world has, however, stuck determinedly to its pictographic form. The adoption of a standard "romanization" (Pinyin) has made teaching and dictionary work easier, but there is little appetite for discarding the characters in favor of Pinyin. This is not simply nostalgia. The Chinese spoken language has far too many words that are spelled exactly the same in Pinyin, and the four tones alone are of limited help in distinguishing these homophones. One entry of the Hunihan database has several hundred words listed under the syllable "ji". As characters they are relatively easy to distinguish; in Pinyin it is impossible.

However, all languages have their special idiosyncrasies. Judgments as to which are the hardest to learn are highly subjective, and are critically affected by individual aptitudes.

Many countries outside Europe are "user-friendly" for the European beginner, having adopted many words, with familiar roots; having little grammar or syntax to worry about, and being written alphabetically. In this respect, Malay must come high on the list of the world's kindest languages, from a beginner's point of view. The language is conveniently peppered with words borrowed from Dutch, Portuguese, Spanish, Arabic, Hindu and English.

But China, unlike Malaysia, has not borrowed and adopted many foreign words, and the question remains whether Chinese deserves its reputation as the most difficult language in the world. There is no denying that it takes a lot longer to learn written Chinese than it does a language with an alphabetical form.

The spoken language does not contain many difficult sounds, but to master the tones, so that you automatically use the right tone for every word, requires drill and time, which few casual students are able to give to the subject. The Chinese have to be particularly patient people to forgive foreigners for torturing their ancient language.

The combination of its pictographic written language with its tones and mass of words that all sound the same, and a vocabulary that has borrowed little from other languages, means that we should certainly allow Chinese a place as one of the world's most difficult language to learn. But when Chinese is judged as a language to use, the situation is different. Once you have learned a character it is quicker to read, however many strokes it has, than a long word in an alphabetical language. The Chinese equivalent of speed writing can be very fast indeed, and there is no need to worry about grammar and syntax. You are embarking on the study of one of the world's oldest and most difficult languages, but it can be fun and highly satisfying to decipher its mysteries.

FURTHER READING

For those who wish to go further into this subject, here are some suggestions. First, there is the Needham multi-volume project, each divided into sub-volumes. The whole set will provide even the most ardent reader with the material for a lifetime worth of study of all things Chinese. The series is entitled "Science and Civilization in China", and the sweep of coverage is unbelievably wide. There are summaries available, and of course there is no need to buy every section.

For dictionaries, there is a large choice. The Shou Wen written about 100 AD, and the Kang Xi Dictionary of the 18th Century provide a solid base of knowledge on the characters used until the late Twentieth Century. The Shuo Wen attempts quite often to explain origins. Among the Chinese Language books of considerable interest are 汉字密码 "Hanzi Mima", two volumes, by Tang Han, published in Shanghai in 2002, and 汉字的故事 "Hanzi de Gushi" by Yu Nairao, published in Beijing in 2005. Both of these books provide excellent examples of the ancient script.

There are many Internet websites about the Chinese language. More are been added regularly. Below are some good resources:

- http://www.zdic.net, the most complete database on Chinese characters (in Chinese only)
- http://www.zhongwen.com, a valuable source of information on the meaning of about six thousand characters (in English)
- http://unicode.org/charts/unihan.html, provides a search interface to the Unicode Hàn (漢) Database (Unihan)
- http://www.pleco.com, comprehensive electronic E↔C dictionary on mobile phone. See http://www.wenlin.com for a PC version (Windows/Mac/Linux)

Good hunting!

考

Definition	To check, give or take an examination
Character Evolution	耂 耂 丂 考
Stroke Order	一 十 土 耂 耂 考
Chinese Proverb	考虑再三

FINAL TEST 1: WRITING

It is your turn now to write each character we have learned. If you have difficulties, refer to the lesson corresponding to the character's sequence number.

1	一		18	点		35	心	
2	二		19	店		36	想	
3	三		20	床		37	日	
4	十		21	去		38	白	
5	人		22	在		39	勺	
6	个		23	王		40	的	
7	大		24	主		41	百	
8	太		25	住		42	是	
9	天		26	国		43	早	
10	从		27	因		44	昨	
11	内		28	木		45	口	
12	肉		29	林		46	喝	
13	土		30	森		47	禾	
14	坐		31	休		48	和	
15	广		32	本		49	香	
16	座		33	目		50	吃	
17	占		34	相		51	品	

52	回	
53	女	
54	了	
55	子	
56	好	
57	安	
58	字	
59	家	
60	妈	
61	吗	
62	骂	
63	石	
64	码	
65	田	
66	力	
67	办	
68	为	
69	男	
70	果	
71	门	

72	们	
73	问	
74	间	
75	买	
76	卖	
77	又	
78	双	
79	友	
80	没	
81	刀	
82	米	
83	来	
84	粉	
85	水	
86	冰	
87	汁	
88	千	
89	开	
90	古	
91	舌	

92	话	
93	活	
94	月	
95	朋	
96	明	
97	有	
98	今	
99	冷	
100	户	
101	万	
102	方	
103	房	
104	上	
105	下	
106	卡	
107	直	
108	具	
109	真	
110	寸	
111	对	

No.	Character	No.	Character	No.	Character
112	过	132	还	152	很
113	时	133	看	153	春
114	村	134	会	154	夏
115	树	135	我	155	秋
116	贝	136	你	156	冬
117	见	137	也	157	鼠
118	贵	138	地	158	牛
119	现	139	他	159	虎
120	立	140	她	160	兔
121	产	141	它	161	龙
122	位	142	东	162	蛇
123	站	143	南	163	马
124	小	144	西	164	羊
125	少	145	北	165	猴
126	尖	146	要	166	鸡
127	夕	147	前	167	狗
128	多	148	后	168	猪
129	名	149	左		
130	句	150	右		
131	不	151	中		

You should now know the characters in the below table. Look at them carefully, they should be familiar to you!

A	四		D	七		G	百	
B	五		E	八		H	万	
C	六		F	九		I	千	

FINAL TEST 2: MEANING

Write the meaning for each character we have learned. If you have difficulties, refer to the lesson corresponding to the character's sequence number.

1	一		12	肉	
2	二		13	土	
3	三		14	坐	
4	十		15	广	
5	人		16	座	
6	个		17	占	
7	大		18	点	
8	太		19	店	
9	天		20	床	
10	从		21	去	
11	内		22	在	

23	王			43	早	
24	主			44	昨	
25	住			45	口	
26	国			46	喝	
27	因			47	禾	
28	木			48	和	
29	林			49	香	
30	森			50	吃	
31	休			51	品	
32	本			52	回	
33	目			53	女	
34	相			54	了	
35	心			55	子	
36	想			56	好	
37	日			57	安	
38	白			58	字	
39	勺			59	家	
40	的			60	妈	
41	百			61	吗	
42	是			62	骂	

63	石		83	来	
64	码		84	粉	
65	田		85	水	
66	力		86	冰	
67	办		87	汁	
68	为		88	千	
69	男		89	开	
70	果		90	古	
71	门		91	舌	
72	们		92	话	
73	问		93	活	
74	间		94	月	
75	买		95	朋	
76	卖		96	明	
77	又		97	有	
78	双		98	今	
79	友		99	冷	
80	没		100	户	
81	刀		101	万	
82	米		102	方	

103	房		123	站	
104	上		124	小	
105	下		125	少	
106	卡		126	尖	
107	直		127	夕	
108	具		128	多	
109	真		129	名	
110	寸		130	句	
111	对		131	不	
112	过		132	还	
113	时		133	看	
114	村		134	会	
115	树		135	我	
116	贝		136	你	
117	见		137	也	
118	贵		138	地	
119	现		139	他	
120	立		140	她	
121	产		141	它	
122	位		142	东	

143	南	
144	西	
145	北	
146	要	
147	前	
148	后	
149	左	
150	右	
151	中	
152	很	
153	春	
154	夏	
155	秋	
156	冬	
157	鼠	
158	牛	
159	虎	
160	兔	
161	龙	
162	蛇	
163	马	

164	羊	
165	猴	
166	鸡	
167	狗	
168	猪	

You now should be able to know what the characters in the below table are. Look at them carefully, they should be familiar to you!

A	四	
B	五	
C	六	
D	七	
E	八	
F	九	
G	十	

If you can't find their meaning, refer to the first page of chapters four to ten.

FINAL TEST 3: RADICALS

Write down the radical of each character and select the correct radical definition. If you have difficulties, refer to the lessons 2 and 8.

#	RADICAL	MEANING	EXAMPLE
1		☐ Food ☐ Man	从
2		☐ Hand ☐ Insect	打
3		☐ Moon ☐ Sun	明
4		☐ Meat ☐ Table	肺
5		☐ Wood ☐ Meat	相
6		☐ Ice ☐ Water	泳
7		☐ Light ☐ Fire	灯
8		☐ Sickness ☐ Container	病
9		☐ Eye ☐ Moon	眼
10		☐ Meat ☐ Flame	朕
11		☐ Music ☐ Insect	蛇
12		☐ Flower ☐ Ice	冰
13		☐ Speech ☐ Travel	讲
14		☐ Knife ☐ Roof	召
15		☐ Mouth ☐ House	否

#	RADICAL	MEANING	EXAMPLE
16		☐ Wood ☐ Animal	犸
17		☐ Water ☐ Language	讯
18		☐ Animal ☐ Root	羚
19		☐ Fish ☐ Language	鲐
20		☐ Plant ☐ House	花
21		☐ Animal ☐ Hair	彪
22		☐ Tree ☐ Animal	驼
23		☐ Sickness ☐ Weather	病
24		☐ Eye ☐ Food	盲
25		☐ Animal ☐ Cloth	狍
26		☐ Animal ☐ Flower	牡
27		☐ Field ☐ Ice	男
28		☐ Roof ☐ Musical instrument	官
29		☐ Liquid ☐ Door	闯
30		☐ Roof ☐ Dancer	家

FINAL TEST 4: PINYIN

For each of the characters in the below table, write down the Pinyin. If you have difficulties, refer to the lesson 10.

#	CHAR	PINYIN	#	CHAR	PINYIN	#	CHAR	PINYIN
1	一		18	点		35	心	
2	二		19	店		36	想	
3	三		20	床		37	日	
4	十		21	去		38	白	
5	人		22	在		39	勺	
6	个		23	王		40	的	
7	大		24	主		41	百	
8	太		25	住		42	是	
9	天		26	国		43	早	
10	从		27	因		44	昨	
11	内		28	木		45	口	
12	肉		29	林		46	喝	
13	土		30	森		47	禾	
14	坐		31	休		48	和	
15	广		32	本		49	香	
16	座		33	目		50	吃	
17	占		34	相		51	品	

#	CHAR	PINYIN	#	CHAR	PINYIN	#	CHAR	PINYIN
52	回		72	们		92	话	
53	女		73	问		93	活	
54	了		74	间		94	月	
55	子		75	买		95	朋	
56	好		76	卖		96	明	
57	安		77	又		97	有	
58	字		78	双		98	今	
59	家		79	友		99	冷	
60	妈		80	没		100	户	
61	吗		81	刀		101	万	
62	骂		82	米		102	方	
63	石		83	来		103	房	
64	码		84	粉		104	上	
65	田		85	水		105	下	
66	力		86	冰		106	卡	
67	办		87	汁		107	直	
68	为		88	千		108	具	
69	男		89	开		109	真	
70	果		90	古		110	寸	
71	门		91	舌		111	对	

#	CHAR	PINYIN	#	CHAR	PINYIN	#	CHAR	PINYIN
112	过		132	还		152	很	
113	时		133	看		153	春	
114	村		134	会		154	夏	
115	树		135	我		155	秋	
116	贝		136	你		156	冬	
117	见		137	也		157	鼠	
118	贵		138	地		158	牛	
119	现		139	他		159	虎	
120	立		140	她		160	兔	
121	产		141	它		161	龙	
122	位		142	东		162	蛇	
123	站		143	南		163	马	
124	小		144	西		164	羊	
125	少		145	北		165	猴	
126	尖		146	要		166	鸡	
127	夕		147	前		167	狗	
128	多		148	后		168	猪	
129	名		149	左				
130	句		150	右				
131	不		151	中				

APPENDIX

LIST OF CHARACTERS ARRANGED ACCORDING TO THEIR MEANING

The following lists refer to the characters in the main lessons. They do not cover the characters in the proverb and zodiac sections, many of which have not been included in the main lessons. Readers should also remember that <u>characters often have a range of meanings</u>; for example, 门 can mean a gate or a door; 信 can mean sincere or believe; 利 can mean sharp or profit; 日 can mean sun or day. The various meaning and concepts conveyed characters are set out in the lessons.

DEFINITION	SIMPLIFIED / TRADITIONAL	CHARACTER NUMBER
A		
Again (once -)	又	77
Also	也	137
Ancient	古	90
And	和	48
Appear	现	119
Appearance	相	34
Article	品	51
Ask (to -)	问	73
Autumn	秋	155
B		

DEFINITION	SIMPLIFIED / TRADITIONAL	CHARACTER NUMBER
Back	后	148
Be able to (to -)	会	134
Beause	因	27
Because of	为	68
Bed	床	20
Before	前	147
Between	间	74
Big	大	7
Buy (to -)	买	75
C		
Calm	安	57

DEFINITION	SIMPLIFIED / TRADITIONAL	CHARACTER NUMBER
Card	卡	106
Center	中	151
Character	字	58
Check (to -)	考	Page 129
Chicken	鸡	166
Clear	明	96
Cold	冷	99
Come (to -)	来	83
Country	国	26
D		
Day	天	9
Direction	方	102
Do (to -)	办	67
Dog	狗	167
Door	门	71
Down	下	105
Dragon	龙	161
Drink (to -)	喝	46
Dusk	夕	127
E		
Early	早	43
Earth	土	13
East	东	142
Eat (to -)	吃	50
Eight	八	Page 100

DEFINITION	SIMPLIFIED / TRADITIONAL	CHARACTER NUMBER
Expensive	贵	118
Experience action marker	过	112
Eye	目	33
F		
Female	女	53
Few	少	125
Field	田	65
Five	五	Page 58
Forest	林	29
Four	四	4
Fragrant	香	49
Friend	友	79
Friend	朋	95
From	从	10
Fruit	果	70
G		
Go (to -)	去	21
Go back (to -)	回	52
Good	好	56
Ground	地	138
H		
Have (to -)	有	97
He	他	139

DEFINITION	SIMPLIFIED / TRADITIONAL	CHARACTER NUMBER
Heart	心	35
Home	家	59
Horse	马	163
House	房	103
Household	户	100
Hundred	百	41
I		
I	我	135
Ice	冰	86
Inch	寸	110
Individual	个	6
Inside	内	11
Is	是	42
It	它	141
J		
Juice	汁	87
K		
King	王	23
Knife	刀	81
L		
Left	左	149
Little (a -)	点	18
Live (to -)	住	25
Live (to -)	活	93
Located at	在	22

DEFINITION	SIMPLIFIED / TRADITIONAL	CHARACTER NUMBER
M		
Male	男	69
Man	人	5
Many	多	128
Master	主	24
Meat	肉	12
Millet	禾	47
Monkey	猴	165
Month	月	94
Mother	妈	60
Mouth	口	45
N		
Name	名	129
Nine	九	Page 109
North	北	145
Not	不	131
Not	没	80
Number	码	64
O		
Occupy (to -)	占	17
Of (possessive)	的	40
One	一	1
Open (to -)	开	89
Ox	牛	158

DEFINITION	SIMPLIFIED / TRADITIONAL	CHARACTER NUMBER
P		
Pig	猪	168
Plural marker for pronouns	们	72
Point (of needle)	尖	126
Position	位	122
Powder	粉	84
Power	力	66
Produce (to -)	产	121
Q		
Question mark	吗	61
Quite	很	152
R		
Rabbit	兔	160
Rat	鼠	157
Really	真	109
Rest (to -)	休	31
Rice	米	82
Right	对	111
Right	右	150
Rock	石	63
Roots	本	32
S		

DEFINITION	SIMPLIFIED / TRADITIONAL	CHARACTER NUMBER
Scold (to -)	骂	62
Seat	座	16
See (to -)	见	117
See (to -)	看	133
Sell (to -)	卖	76
Sentence	句	130
Seven	七	Page 86
She	她	140
Sheep	羊	164
Shellfish	贝	116
Shop	店	19
Sit (to -)	坐	14
Six	六	Page 71
Small	小	124
Snake	蛇	162
Son	子	55
South	南	143
Spoon	勺	39
Spring	春	153
Standing	立	120
Station	站	123
Still	还	132
Straight	直	107
Summer	夏	154
Sun	日	37
T		
Ten	十	Page 114

DEFINITION	SIMPLIFIED / TRADITIONAL	CHARACTER NUMBER	DEFINITION	SIMPLIFIED / TRADITIONAL	CHARACTER NUMBER
Ten thousand	万	101	Two	双	78
Tense Particle	了	54	**U**		
Thicket	森	30	Up	上	104
Think (to -)	想	36	Use (to -)	用	Page 129
Thousand	千	88	**V**		
Three	三	3	Village	村	114
Tiger	虎	159	**W**		
Time	时	113	Want (to -)	要	146
Today	今	98	Water	水	85
Tongue	舌	91	West	西	144
Too	太	8	White	白	38
Tool	具	108	Wide	广	15
Tree	树	115	Winter	冬	156
Tree	木	28	Word	话	92
Two	二	2	**Y**		
			Yesterday	昨	44
			You	你	136

Table 14: List of characters arranged according to their meaning

LIST OF CHARACTERS ARRANGED BY NUMBER OF STROKES

The table below lists the characters we have studied, sorted by number of strokes. As this book focuses on the simplified set of Chinese characters instead of the traditional set, we have listed the simplified version.

NUMBER OF STROKES	CHARACTER	PINYIN	CHARACTER NUMBER	NUMBER OF STROKES	CHARACTER	PINYIN	CHARACTER NUMBER
1	一	yī	1	2	了	liǎo	54
2	七	qī	Page 86	2	二	èr	2
2	九	jiǔ	Page 109	2	人	rén	5

NUMBER OF STROKES	CHARACTER	PINYIN	CHARACTER NUMBER	NUMBER OF STROKES	CHARACTER	PINYIN	CHARACTER NUMBER
2	八	bā	Page 100	4	从	cóng	10
2	刀	dāo	81	4	六	liù	Page 71
2	力	lì	66	4	内	nèi	11
2	十	shì	Page 114	4	办	bàn	67
3	万	wàn	101	4	友	yǒu	79
3	三	sān	3	4	双	shuāng	78
3	上	hōng	104	4	天	tiān	9
3	下	xià	105	4	太	tài	8
3	个	gè	6	4	少	shǎo	125
3	也	yě	137	4	开	kāi	89
3	勺	sháo	39	4	心	xīn	35
3	千	qiān	88	4	户	hù	100
3	口	kǒu	45	4	方	fāng	102
3	土	tǔ	13	4	日	rì	37
3	大	dà	7	4	月	yuè	94
3	女	nǚ	53	4	木	mù	28
3	子	zǐ	55	4	水	shuǐ	85
3	寸	cùn	110	4	牛	niú	158
3	小	xiǎo	124	4	王	wáng	23
3	广	guǎng	15	4	见	jiàn	117
3	门	mén	71	4	贝	bèi	116
3	马	mǎ	163	5	东	dōng	142
3	夕	xī	127	5	主	zhǔ	24
4	不	bù	131	5	他	tā	139
4	中	zhōng	151	5	们	men	72
4	为	wèi	68	5	冬	dōng	156
4	五	wǔ	Page 58	5	北	běi	145
4	今	jīn	98	5	占	zhān	17

NUMBER OF STROKES	CHARACTER	PINYIN	CHARACTER NUMBER	NUMBER OF STROKES	CHARACTER	PINYIN	CHARACTER NUMBER
5	卡	qiǎ	106	6	回	huí	52
5	去	qù	21	6	因	yīn	27
5	古	gǔ	90	6	在	zài	22
5	句	jù	130	6	地	dì	138
5	右	yòu	150	6	多	duō	128
5	四	sì	4	6	她	tā	140
5	它	tā	141	6	好	hǎo	56
5	对	duì	111	6	妈	mā	60
5	左	zuǒ	149	6	字	zì	58
5	本	běn	32	6	安	ān	57
5	汁	zhī	87	6	尖	jiān	126
5	田	tián	65	6	早	zǎo	43
5	白	bái	38	6	有	yǒu	97
5	目	mù	33	6	百	bǎi	41
5	石	shí	63	6	米	mǐ	82
5	禾	hé	47	6	舌	shé	91
5	立	lì	120	6	考	kǎo	Page 139
5	龙	lóng	161	7	位	wèi	122
5	用	yòng	Page 129	7	住	zhù	25
6	买	mǎi	75	7	你	nǐ	136
6	产	chǎn	121	7	冷	lěng	99
6	休	xiū	31	7	坐	zuò	14
6	会	huì	134	7	床	chuáng	20
6	冰	bīng	86	7	我	wǒ	135
6	吃	chī	50	7	时	shí	113
6	名	míng	129	7	村	cūn	114
6	后	hòu	148	7	来	lái	83
6	吗	ma	61	7	没	méi	80

NUMBER OF STROKES	CHARACTER	PINYIN	CHARACTER NUMBER	NUMBER OF STROKES	CHARACTER	PINYIN	CHARACTER NUMBER
7	男	nán	69	9	昨	zuó	44
7	还	huán	132	9	是	shì	42
7	间	jiān	74	9	树	shù	115
7	鸡	jī	166	9	活	huó	93
8	兔	tù	160	9	点	diǎn	18
8	具	jù	108	9	相	xiāng	34
8	卖	mài	76	9	看	kàn	133
8	和	hé	48	9	秋	qiū	155
8	国	guó	26	9	要	yào	146
8	店	diàn	19	9	贵	guì	118
8	房	fáng	103	9	香	xiāng	49
8	明	míng	96	9	骂	mà	62
8	朋	péng	95	10	夏	xià	154
8	林	lín	29	10	家	jiā	59
8	果	guǒ	70	10	座	zuò	16
8	狗	gǒu	167	10	真	zhēn	109
8	现	xiàn	119	10	站	zhàn	123
8	的	de	40	10	粉	fěn	84
8	直	zhí	107	11	猪	zhū	168
8	码	mǎ	64	11	蛇	shé	162
8	虎	hǔ	159	12	森	sēn	30
8	话	huà	92	12	猴	hóu	165
9	前	qián	147	12	喝	hē	46
9	南	nán	143	13	想	xiǎng	36
9	品	pǐn	51	13	鼠	shǔ	157
9	很	hěn	152				
9	春	chūn	153				

Table 15: List of characters arranged by number of strokes

LIST OF 214 KANGXI RADICALS

The following is a list of all 214 Kangxi radicals, used originally in the 1615 Zihui and adopted by the 1716 Kangxi dictionary, in order of the number of strokes along with some examples of characters containing them. This list has become such a common standard that sometimes radicals are referred to by number alone. A reference to "radical 61", for example, without additional context, means 心.

```
一 丨 丶 丿 乙 亅 二 亠 人 儿 入 八 冂 冖 冫 几
凵 刀 力 勹 匕 匚 匸 十 卜 卩 厂 厶 又 口 囗 土
士 夂 夊 夕 大 女 子 宀 寸 小 尢 尸 屮 山 巛 工
己 巾 干 幺 广 廴 廾 弋 弓 彐 彡 彳 心 戈 戶 手
支 攴 文 斗 斤 方 无 日 曰 月 木 欠 止 歹 殳 毋
比 毛 氏 气 水 火 爪 父 爻 爿 片 牙 牛 犬 玄 玉
瓜 瓦 甘 生 用 田 疋 疒 癶 白 皮 皿 目 矛 矢 石
示 禸 禾 穴 立 竹 米 糸 缶 网 羊 羽 老 而 耒 耳
聿 肉 臣 自 至 臼 舌 舛 舟 艮 色 艸 虍 虫 血 行
衣 襾 見 角 言 谷 豆 豕 豸 貝 赤 走 足 身 車 辛
辰 辵 邑 酉 釆 里 金 長 門 阜 隶 隹 雨 青 非 面
革 韋 韭 音 頁 風 飛 食 首 香 馬 骨 高 髟 鬥 鬯
鬲 鬼 魚 鳥 鹵 鹿 麥 麻 黃 黍 黑 黹 黽 鼎 鼓 鼠
鼻 齊 齒 龍 龜 龠


彡 厂 乚 乁 亻 刂 几 勹 卜 巳 屮 丷 兀 尢 母 糸 阝 飠
尢 允 氵 冈 彐 丬 扌 王 礻 龷 申 车 示 辶 辶 阝 飠
乡 彳 氺 罓 虍 长 马 龜 衤 辵 贝 页 风 龟 齐
钅 犭 灬 覀 衤 马 黾 龙 鱼 鸟 卤 黄 齿 龙
```

List of Unicode 'radicals' (AR PL UKai TW)

214 Kangxi radicals and variants based on the traditional Chinese character set

Note:

The stroke count in the following table is based on the traditional Chinese set of characters. Of 214 radicals, 24 have been simplified.

NO.	RADICAL (VARIANTS)	STROKE COUNT	PĪNYĪN	MEANING	EXAMPLES
96	[玉]王 (⺩)	5	yù (wáng)	jade (king)	王玉主弄皇理差圣

(⺩) : Variant

王 : Simplified Chinese

[玉] : Traditional Chinese

NO.	RADICAL (VARIANTS)	STROKE COUNT	PĪNYĪN	MEANING	EXAMPLES
1	一	1	yī	one	七三不世
2	丨	1	gǔn	line	中
3	丶	1	zhǔ	dot	丸主
4	丿	1	piě	slash	久之乎
5	乛 (乙, 乁, 乚)	1	yǐ	second	九也
6	亅	1	jué	hook	了事
7	二	2	èr	two	五井些亚
8	亠	2	tóu	lid	亡交京
9	人(亻)	2	rén	man, human	仁休位今
10	儿	2	ér	legs, son	兄元
11	入	2	rù	enter	入两
12	八	2	bā	eight	公六共兵
13	冂	2	jiōng	open country	内再
14	冖	2	mī	cover	冗冠
15	冫	2	bīng	ice	冬冶冷冻
16	几	2	jī	table	凡
17	凵	2	qǔ	container, open mouth	凶出函
18	刀(刂)	2	dāo	knife, sword	刀分切初利刻则前

NO.	RADICAL (VARIANTS)	STROKE COUNT	PĪNYĪN	MEANING	EXAMPLES
19	力	2	lì	power, force	力加助勉
20	勹	2	bāo	wrap, embrace	勾包
21	匕	2	bǐ	spoon	化北
22	匚	2	fāng	box	匣
23	匸	2	xǐ	hiding enclosure	匹区
24	十	2	shí	ten, complete	十午半博
25	卜	2	bǔ	divination	占卦
26	卩	2	jié	seal	印危卵
27	厂	2	hàn, chǎng	cliff	厚原
28	厶	2	sī	private	去参
29	又	2	yòu	again	友反取受
30	口	3	kǒu	mouth, opening	口古可名君否吴告周味命和哲唐善器
31	囗	3	wéi	enclosure	四回国图
32	土	3	tǔ	earth	土在地型城场壁压
33	士	3	shì	scholar, bachelor	士壹
34	夂	3	zhǐ	go	(夂)
35	夊	3	suī	go slowly	夏
36	夕	3	xī	evening, sunset	夕外多夜
37	大	3	dà	big, very	大天奈奥
38	女	3	nǚ	woman, female	女好妄妻姊始姓姬
39	子	3	zǐ	child, seed	子孔字学
40	宀	3	mián	roof	守家寒实
41	寸	3	cùn	thumb, inch	寸寺尊将
42	小	3	xiǎo	small, insignificant	小少
43	尢, 尣	3	wāng	lame	就
44	尸	3	shī	corpse	尺局
45	屮	3	chè	sprout	屯
46	山	3	shān	mountain	山冈岩岛

NO.	RADICAL (VARIANTS)	STROKE COUNT	PĪNYĪN	MEANING	EXAMPLES
47	巛 (川, 巜)	3	chuān	river	川州巡
48	工	3	gōng	work	工左巫差
49	己 巳 已 巴	3	jǐ	oneself	己巴
50	巾	3	jīn	turban, scarf	市布帝常
51	干	3	gān	dry	平年
52	幺	3	yāo	short, tiny	幻幼
53	广	3	guǎng	sloping roof, wide, broad	序店府度座庭 广厅
54	廴	3	yín	long stride	延
55	廾	3	gǒng	two hands, twenty	弁
56	弋	3	yì	shoot, arrow	式弑
57	弓	3	gōng	bow	弓引弟弱弥
58	彐 (彑)	3	jì	pig snout	象
59	彡	3	shān	bristle, beard	形彦
60	彳	3	chì	step	役彼后得德徵
61	心 (忄小)	4	xīn	heart	必忙忌性悪 情想
62	戈	4	gē	spear, halberd	成式弑戰
63	戶, 户, 戸	4	hù	door, house	戶戻所
64	手 (扌手)	4	shǒu	hand	手持挂举拜拳 掌擊举(打批技 抱押)
65	支	4	zhī	branch	竑敁
66	攴 (攵)	4	pū	rap	收叙数戮
67	文	4	wén	script, literature	文斋学斌斐 斑斓
68	斗	4	dǒu	dipper	料斡
69	斤	4	jīn	axe	所斧新斥斩 断
70	方	4	fāng	square	方放旅族
71	无	4	wú	not	无旡既旤

NO.	RADICAL (VARIANTS)	STROKE COUNT	PĪNYĪN	MEANING	EXAMPLES
72	日	4	rì	sun, day	日白百明的映时晚
73	曰	4	yuē	say	书最晋曷曹曾
74	月	4	yuè	moon, month	有服青朝
75	木	4	mù	tree	木杏板相根森楽机末本杉林
76	欠	4	qiàn	lack, yawn	欣钦欧欲歌
77	止	4	zhǐ	stop	正步此步武歪岁
78	歹 (歺)	4	dǎi	death, decay	死列殡
79	殳	4	shū	weapon, lance	役投殴殷
80	毋(母)	4	wú	mother, do not	毋母每姆梅
81	比	4	bǐ	compare, compete	皆批毕毖毗毚
82	毛	4	máo	fur, hair	毡毡毦毫氅耗
83	氏	4	shì	clan	氏民纸婚氓
84	气	4	qì	steam, breath	氘汽氧
85	水 (氵,氺)	4	shuǐ	water	水永泳决治海演汉瀬
86	火 (灬)	4	huǒ	fire	火灯毯爆(烈烹焦然煮)
87	爪 (爫)	4	zhǎo	claw	爬再争爰为
88	父	4	fù	father	斧釜
89	爻	4	yáo	mix, twine, cross	爼爽尔
90	爿	4	qiáng	split wood	床奘牒
91	片	4	piàn	slice	版牌牒
92	牙	4	yá	fang	芽呀掙
93	牛 (牜)	4	niú	cow	告牟牧物特解
94	犬 (犭)	4	quǎn	dog	犬犯狂狙狗献獸

NO.	RADICAL (VARIANTS)	STROKE COUNT	PĪNYĪN	MEANING	EXAMPLES
95	玄	5	xuán	dark, profound	弦兹
96	[玉]王 (王)	5	yù (wáng)	jade (king)	王 玉 主 弄 皇 理 差 圣
97	瓜	5	guā	melon	呱 瓞
98	瓦	5	wǎ	tile	瓩 瓮 甄
99	甘	5	gān	sweet	柑 甜 酣
100	生	5	shēng	life	牲 笙 甥
101	用 (甩)	5	yòng	use	佣 甫 宁
102	田	5	tián	field	田 町 思 留 略 番
103	疋 (𤴓)	5	pǐ	bolt of cloth	疏 楚 胥 延
104	疒	5	chuáng	sickness	病 症 痛 癌 癖
105	癶	5	bō	dotted tent	発 登
106	白	5	bái	white	兜 的 皆 皇
107	皮	5	pí	skin	拔 彼 波
108	皿	5	mǐn	dish	盂 盃 盉 监 蘯
109	目	5	mù	eye	目 见 具 省 眠 眼 观 览
110	矛	5	máo	spear	茅 矜
111	矢	5	shǐ	arrow	医 族 矩
112	石	5	shí	stone	石 岩 砂 破 碑 碧
113	示 (礻)	5	shì	spirit, ancestor	示 礼 社 奈 神 祭 视 禁 福
114	内	5	róu	track	禹 禺 禽
115	禾	5	hé	grain	利 私 季 和 科 香 秦 谷
116	穴	5	xué	cave	空 突 宵 窘 窝 窭 窦
117	立	5	lì	stand, erect	立 音 产 竖 意 新 端 亲 竞
118	竹 (⺮)	6	zhú	bamboo	竺 笑 第 等 简
119	米	6	mǐ	rice	料 断 奥 糊 麟

NO.	RADICAL (VARIANTS)	STROKE COUNT	PĪNYĪN	MEANING	EXAMPLES
120	[糸] 纟(纟)	6	sī	silk	系 级 纸 素 细 组 终 绘 紫
121	缶	6	fǒu	jar	缶 缸 窑 陶
122	网 (罒, 皿, 冈, 宀)	6	wǎng	net	买 罪 置 罗
123	羊 (羊)	6	yáng	sheep	着 羚 翔 着
124	羽	6	yǔ	feather	习 翀 翁 翔
125	老 (耂)	6	lǎo	old	耆 孝 耄
126	而	6	ér	and, but	耎 耐 耑
127	耒	6	lěi	plow	耔 粗 耦 耰
128	耳	6	ěr	ear	取 闻 职 丛
129	聿 (聿)	6	yù	brush	律 书 建
130	肉 (月)	6	ròu	meat	肉 肖 股 胃 腠 脎
131	臣	6	chén	minster, official	卧 宦 藏
132	自	6	zì	self	自 臮 臬 臲
133	至	6	zhì	arrive	致 銍 台
134	臼	6	jiù	mortar	柏 舅 舂 鼠 插
135	舌	6	shé	tongue	乱 适 话 舍
136	舛	6	chuǎn	opposite	舛 舜 舞
137	舟	6	zhōu	boat	航 船 舰
138	艮	6	gēn	stopping	良 饮 很
139	色	6	sè	color, prettiness	色 艳 艳
140	艸 (艹)	6	cǎo	grass	共 花 英 苦 草 茶 落 幕 靴 鞄 藥
141	虍	6	hǔ	tiger	虎 虐 彪 虒
142	虫	6	chóng	insect	蚯 蚓 强 触 蚁 蟹
143	血	6	xuè	blood	洫 盍 衃 众
144	行	6	xíng	go, do	行 衍 术 冲
145	衣 (衤)	6	yī	clothes	衣 初 被 装 裁 复

NO.	RADICAL (VARIANTS)	STROKE COUNT	PĪNYĪN	MEANING	EXAMPLES
146	西 (覀, 襾)	6	xī	west	西 要 覊
147	[見]见	7	jiàn	see	规 亲 觉 观
148	角	7	jiǎo	horn	觚 解 粗 觥 触
149	[言]讠 (訁)	7	yán	speech	誵 訊 诏 评 詞 諙 试 謷
150	谷	7	gǔ	valley	溪 磎 裕
151	豆	7	dòu	bean	豈 丰 竖
152	豕	7	shǐ	pig	豕 豚 象
153	豸	7	zhì	cat, badger	豹 貌 猫 豺 貉
154	[貝]贝	7	bèi	shell	财 贼 赐 赣 贫 货 贯 贸
155	赤	7	chì	red, naked	赫 赭
156	走 (赱)	7	zǒu	run	赴 起 超
157	足(⻊)	7	zú	foot	跑 跨 跟 跪 路
158	身	7	shēn	body	躬 躲 躯
159	[車]车	7	chē	cart, car	轨 软 较 军 载
160	辛	7	xīn	bitter	辜 辟 辣 办 辨
161	辰	7	chén	morning	辱 农
162	辵 (辶, 辶, 辶)	7	chuò / zouzhi	walk	巡 迎 通 追 逃 辶 迎 进
163	邑 (阝)	7	yì	town (阝 right)	那 邦 郎 部 郭 都 乡
164	酉	7	yǒu	wine, alcohol	醉 酱 油 醒 酸
165	釆	7	biàn	divide, distinguish, choose	釉 释
166	里	7	lǐ	village, mile	野 野
167	金 ([釒]钅)	8	jīn	metal, gold	银 铜 钉 锐 鏗 锴 鈺 铋 钳 钟 铰
168	[長]长 (镸)	8	cháng	long, grow	镸 镽
169	[門]门	8	mén	gate	间 闲 关 閗 闭 开 闰 间 关

NO.	RADICAL (VARIANTS)	STROKE COUNT	PĪNYĪN	MEANING	EXAMPLES
170	阜 (阝)	8	fù	mound, dam (阝 left)	阪 防 阻 陆 陉 院 险 陈
171	隶	8	lì	slave, capture	隶 隺
172	隹	8	zhuī	small bird	雀 集 雁 难 雀 雅
173	雨	8	yǔ	rain	雾 霜 雪 霸 雪 云 雾
174	青, 靑	8	qīng	blue	靖 靖 静
175	非	8	fēi	wrong	靠 靠 辈
176	面 (靣)	9	miàn	face	腼 靥
177	革	9	gé	leather, rawhide	靴 鞍 鞅 鞍 鞭
178	[韋]韦	9	wéi	tanned leather	韦 韩 韬
179	韭	9	jiǔ	leek	韱 韲
180	音	9	yīn	sound	韶 韵 馨
181	[頁]页	9	yè	leaf	项 项 顺 须 领 头 颓 顶
182	[風]风	9	fēng	wind	台 飘 飙 飚 飌
183	[飛]飞	9	fēi	fly	飜 飝
184	食 ([飠]饣)	9	shí	eat, food	饭 饮 饿 余 餐 养
185	首	9	shǒu	head	馗 馘
186	香	9	xiāng	fragrance	馨 馫
187	[馬]马	10	mǎ	horse	冯 驯 驰 驻 惊
188	骨	10	gǔ	bone	骼 胼 髀 骷 鲠
189	[高]高	10	gāo	tall	䯁 䯂
190	髟	10	biāo	long hair	发 须 松 胡 髦
191	[鬥]斗	10	dòu	fight	闹 鬪
192	鬯	10	chàng	herbs, sacrificial wine	郁 郁
193	鬲	10	lì	tripod, cauldron	鬶 鬷 鬴
194	鬼	10	guǐ	ghost, demon	魂 魁 魃 魄
195	鱼	11	yú	fish	鲤 鲍 鲂 鱿 鲗 鲄 魟 鲀
196	[鳥]鸟	11	niǎo	bird	鸠 鸡 鸩 凤 鸣 鸪 鸡 鸣 鸿 鸳

NO.	RADICAL (VARIANTS)	STROKE COUNT	PĪNYĪN	MEANING	EXAMPLES
197	[鹵] 卤	11	lǔ	salt	咸 碱 盐
198	鹿	11	lù	deer	尘 麃 麇 麗 麟
199	[麥] 麦	11	mài	wheat	麴 面 麱 麨 麪
200	麻	11	má	hemp, flax	幺 麾
201	黄	12	huáng	yellow	難 黉
202	黍	12	shǔ	millet	黏 黎
203	黑	12	hēi	black	点 黛 黱 党
204	黹	12	zhǐ	embroidery, needle-work	黼 黻
205	[黽] 黾	13	mǐn	frog, amphibian	鳖 鼋 鼍
206	鼎	13	dǐng	tripod	鼏 鼐
207	鼓	13	gǔ	drum	鼗 鼟
208	鼠	13	shǔ	rat, mouse	鼢 鼩 鼩
209	鼻	14	bí	nose	鼽 鼽 鼽
210	[齊] 齐	14	qí	even, uniformly	斋 斎 斎
211	[齒] 齿	15	chǐ	tooth, molar	龄 龆 龂
212	[龍] 龙	16	lóng	dragon	龘 龗
213	[龜] 龟	16	guī	turtle, tortoise	龝
214	龠	17	yuè	flute	龢 龥

Table 16: List of 214 Kangxi Radicals

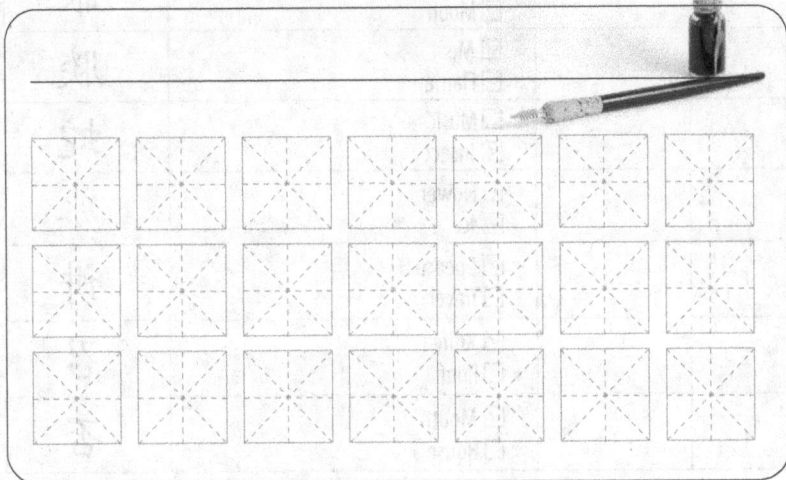

TEST ANSWER KEY 1

Test answer key for "Lesson Two: Test 1" on page 30.

#	RADICAL	MEANING	EXAMPLE
1		☐ Food ☑ Man	从
2		☑ Hand ☐ Insect	打
3		☐ Moon ☑ Sun	明
4		☑ Meat ☐ Table	肺
5		☑ Wood ☐ Meat	相
6		☐ Ice ☑ Water	泳
7		☐ Light ☑ Fire	灯
8		☑ Sickness ☐ Container	病
9		☑ Eye ☐ Moon	眼
10		☑ Meat ☐ Flame	朕
11		☐ Music ☑ Insect	蛇
12		☐ Flower ☑ Ice	冰
13		☑ Speech ☐ Travel	讲
14		☑ Knife ☐ Roof	召
15		☑ Mouth ☐ House	否

TEST ANSWER KEY 2

Test answer key for "Lesson Eight: Test 1" on page 106
Note: for entries #1 to #15 refer to the table "Test Answer Key 1" on page 171.

#	RADICAL	MEANING	EXAMPLE
16		☐ Wood ☑ Animal	犸
17		☐ Water ☑ Language	讯
18		☑ Animal ☐ Root	羚
19		☑ Fish ☐ Language	鲐
20		☑ Plant ☐ House	花
21		☐ Animal ☑ Hair	彪
22		☐ Tree ☑ Animal	驼
23		☑ Sickness ☐ Weather	病
24		☑ Eye ☐ Food	盲
25		☑ Animal ☐ Cloth	狍
26		☑ Animal ☐ Flower	牡
27		☑ Field ☐ Ice	男
28		☑ Roof ☐ Musical instrument	官
29		☐ Liquid ☑ Door	闯
30		☑ Roof ☐ Dancer	家

Discovery Publisher is a multimedia publisher whose mission is to inspire and support personal transformation, spiritual growth and awakening. We strive with every title to preserve the essential wisdom of the author, spiritual teacher, thinker, healer, and visionary artist.